BLIND SPOTS in Relationships

What I don't know I don't know about myself

JERRY D. CLARK, LPC

Published by : Jerry D Clark, LPC
ISBN: 978-0-578-34780-6

design | layout : kel majors | kelgraphix@gmail.com

Visit author site : www.jerrydclark.com

BL.IND SPTS

Relati●nships

What I don't know I don't know about myself

This book belongs | has been given to

_____

Keep looking for the blind spots!

DEDICATION

George Pulliam, my mentor, my teacher, my friend: the man who taught me to be gently curious, to always be open to possibilities, to look for the best in everyone I meet, and the greatest answer to any question is *"It depends,"* because it does.

Rest in peace my friend. You will be forever in my mind as I address people who seek guidance. Your words will go with me forever.

CONTENTS

Preface

Why does this always happen to me?

Blind spots...man, what are they?

For me, it is employing automatic and unconscious habits, actions, or behaviors without being aware of their consequences. It is exhibiting behaviors or actions that are unappealing to others but are not in my awareness, nor can I hear others when they attempt to warn me of their negative impact to my likability and success.

This is not a book of advice but a book of possibilities.

Blind spots are gold mines. Trust me, I have been completely unaware of these destructive habits and behaviors which were causing me problems in relationships.

Discovering and overcoming these hidden blind spots has improved my communication skills and allowed me the closeness in relationships I was looking for, yet it was so foreign to me. Be careful. If closeness is foreign to you, you could be the one sabotaging it. Sometimes vulnerability can be frightening until you employ the courage it takes to accept it.

The possibilities are endless and if you choose to follow any of the ideas presented in this book, success will depend on understanding and practicing them. I pray you will gain richness and success in improving your life, relationships, and coaching the ones you so dearly love.

Look for the blind spots!

rigin
Growing up

San Angelo was a laid-back town and living outside the town was even more laid back.

Having grown up in West Texas and being the fifth of six children, we were not taught a lot about emotional intelligence or healthy relationships. Having an older brother, three older sisters and a younger brother, it was customary to tease the younger ones.

> **Unbeknownst to them, sarcasm and belittling
> was a *confidence thief.***

We grew up in a very humble family. We did not want for much, but we did not have much either. Mom and Dad were extremely generous and gave all they had, but could not give what they did not get. There was very little evidence of healthy relationships and emotional maturity. It was more about survival, education and doing better than they had done.

I loved my parents dearly and lost them in the early 90's. They were extremely loving, giving and wanted us to succeed. No one will ever know the sacrifices they made for us.

Growing up in the 50's was a great time of change for the better. We were among the baby boomers. I can remember when we got our first TV and how I thought we had moved so far up technologically.

I was remarkably close to Dad and Mom. Mom introduced me to Jesus and the Bible. Dad taught me how to work. Displays of weak emotions were not allowed in our house. We were taught not to cry. I certainly do not hold this against them; I know they did their best. It was just the emotional education, or lack thereof, in which they were trained.

My first four years of education were in a two-room schoolhouse in

Tankersley, Texas. The first, second, and third grades were in one room and the fourth, fifth and sixth were in another. It sounds like this was exceptionally long ago, but it seems like only yesterday.

I remember the 5th grade; I went to David Crockett Elementary School in San Angelo. I thought this was nifty because they had three fifth grade classes, three fifth grade teachers and a football team. I excelled in football and was not so interested in academics. I played football in junior high, but was too small to play in high school. Just out of high school, I attended San Angelo College for two semesters and then joined the Marine Corps in 1966. I spent two years in the Marine Corps, thirteen months in Vietnam.

My experience in the Marines did not enhance my emotional intelligence; in fact, it probably stunted it more. I excelled in the Marines. I already knew how to keep my emotions hidden and knew how to work hard with little effort. My emotional immaturity was even worse coming back from Vietnam. After the Marines, I returned to Angelo State University, got married and graduated in 1971 with a BBA, I started to work in engineering for General Telephone Company.

Having no emotional education or training at home and returning from the warped emotional training I received in the Marines, I was ill-equipped to be married, much less become a dad. We had two wonderful sons, and I regret to say that my ability to be a successful father was extremely lacking.

I knew the importance of discipline and respect; ask my boys, I treated them as though they were recruits in boot camp. I loved them dearly and was so proud to be their dad, but as incredibly young boys, I held them to excessively high standards.

As I look back, I regret this part of my journey so much. There is a balance in calling one to their excellence or breaking their spirit.

> **Ill-equipped to be a husband or a dad,
> has fueled the evolution of this book.**

Not knowing how to effectively express emotions, share feelings, or have any kind of emotional maturity, caused me to push through life at work and at home as though I was still in the Corps. In retrospect, this caused success at work but created terrible shame and misery at home. Our marriage failed after 13 years. I still remember the horrible experience of telling our boys.

I remarried two years later and lo and behold, created the same kind of family I had in my previous marriage. *(Not surprised, huh?)* It was not until I seriously went to counseling that I began to see the blind spots that were generating extreme difficulties in my relationships with the ones I love so much. I joined a men's group and a couples' group. I was right, in control, and could rationalize, minimize, and justify most everything. I could not understand why the women in the couples' group did not like me. *(Imagine that?!)* It took so much self-reflection and introspective work. I had to go through another boot camp…the emotional one. It was amazing when I began to see what the group members were telling me; my life got simpler and easier.

They were actually being kind in their endeavor to help me. What I heard was criticism, blaming and shaming—I did not want to see it as my fault—I had had enough while growing up and in the Corps. I began to research "emotions." I really did not know I had them. I think prior to this, I had only two…happy and mad.

I had no idea I was controlling.

I had no idea I was angry.

I had no idea I was so demanding, and that I had to be right all the time. On top of that, I despised feeling controlled, wrong, and shamed.

I did not recognize that I was relaying these feelings to the ones I loved. **(Ouch, that hurts)** *Emotional maturity was creeping in. Thank you, Lord.*

How terribly embarrassing to admit my behavior towards my family. It was all a result of where I had been, what I had/had not learned, and what I wanted to demonstrate. I was beginning to see so many negative blind spots and I began to work on change.

I wanted to learn to be gentler to myself. I wanted to tame my emotions rather than have them run my life. *(Anxiety up...intellect down)* I wanted to be assertive but kinder and more sympathetic to the ones I loved. I wanted to be more understanding, to listen better, to appreciate other's ideas, help others feel right and safe in my presence. It took a while to create this kind of change. I wanted inner peace and I found it. I wanted to let go of the baggage of my past and look forward to the future.

In counseling, I began hearing God call me back to college to become a counselor. It was not an audible voice but a compassionate tug. I was concerned about being successful. I kept hearing God's whisper,

*"Take care of my people and
I will take care of you".*

I was witnessing first-hand the effectiveness of counseling for individuals and families and desperately wanted to be involved.

Go back to school?

I did not know how this could happen. I needed eighteen prerequisite undergraduate hours in psychology and sixty postgraduate hours. After that, I had to complete an internship, 3,000 hours of supervised counseling, of which required 1,500 hours spent in direct contact with individuals, groups, or families. In addition to this, I was working full time as an Engineering and Construction Manager in the telecommunications industry.

I knew I heard God, so I started back to school with the idea that my grades would be the deciding factor of continuing the process. The grades came easily. It took a huge commitment to go back to college and get a master's degree in Marriage and Family Therapy.

It was all worth it.

I have had an extraordinarily successful practice since 1996. I love working with people, especially people who desire to have something much better than what they have been experiencing. Spending time talking to families, individuals, teenagers, or children has brought to the forefront that I repeat the same counsel over and over so many times. I want to share the possibilities with more people, so you too have the opportunity to grow and be successful in your relationships.

It's going to take action and hard work, so dig in and enjoy!

Blinds Spots

Where it all started...

I had graduated college, been to war, had a fine thirty-year corporate career in telecommunications, a great twenty-five years of counseling.

In the early nineties, I was in a second marriage with my two sons and a stepson. Life seemed to be working for me, yet I was in hesitation. I had great people in my life, but I was lonely.

Life was not complete.

Where were the ones, I desired to have the most? Did I cut myself from the herd or did others cut me? Regardless of the answer, I felt alone.

I was a nice guy.

I knew I was a good provider.

I did many great things for the ones I love and for others.

Still, I felt disconnected and alone.

Where did I go wrong?

I recognized my close relationships were distant and unhealthy but could not understand or appreciate the root cause. It was easy to recognize something was wrong and not look inward but outward to see what others were doing that cause me this detachment. It was easier to blame and see the source being another's issue, rather than me being at fault or erring in some way.

When I blame, I do not need to change.

Locating my blind spots required courage and a desire to build a better me. I had to be willing to change to be able to experience full, enjoyable, and healthy relationships.

As I mentioned, I was very controlling and did not know it. I was called *Mister Perfect, Mister Right, Know-It-All,* and *Controller.* I felt I was always *"in the know."* By being *"in the know"* and not wanting to have any faults, I did not see this as unflattering or a problem. It was clear it was someone else's issue. They just could not live up to my standards. Looking back, I could rationalize, minimize, and justify anything. [BLIND SPOT]

What an awful actualization as I write these words today, but it was true. I could not hear what I did not want to hear. I did not realize or value feedback that was essential to equip me with exactly what I needed. It was as if my imperfections, blunders, and blemishes were blinding me of these feelings of being unacceptable, unworthy, or incapable. I could not see how this powerful feedback would make me more likable and successful. I so drastically needed it, but I was in opposition to this kind of *"perceived"* criticism and how would it give me an opportunity to build a better me later in life.

Hearing negative things about me awakened shame. Shame was a monster that kept me from looking inward to improve my life and my close relationships.

Shame was a difficult thing for me to endure. To be told I was doing something wrong or out of line was impossible to hear.

Listening to grow was an unfamiliar concept.

I did not think I needed to hear negative things about myself. Why don't they look at what I have done well?

Why do they focus on my negatives?

It is easier to blame others rather than look at myself. When I am open to hearing about myself, I can overcome these kinds of blind spots. Now I hear them as opportunities and ways of effectively connecting. What a wonderful experience; I now have the courage to be vulnerable. I can now laugh at myself. This is something that has become so powerful for me. I saw vulnerability as intense weakness. What a terrible misconception.

Today, I am grateful for this kind of feedback. It can only make me better. If I want to live out my life with the fewest regrets possible, I must have this kind of feedback to give me that chance.

Change requires an inordinate amount of courage.

Courage to be vulnerable.

Courage to accept my faults, blemishes, and inability to have the kind of life I want.

Courage to change me, even when others aren't acting the way I want.

I have discovered changing other people is next to impossible. I can influence change, but I cannot change them. When I stop blaming and start looking at my contribution to the condition of the relationship and the family, hope begins to manifest itself. Change requires self-discipline, openness, insane fortitude, and confidence to know that hard work will bring me what I'm looking for.

Will it be hard? Yes!

Will it be worth it? Absolutely!

I need to do something different so I can have the ones who are close to me in my life. Close—meaning tangible, connected, in communication with, and participating in life together.

When I change my actions and behaviors, I notice it's easier for others to begin to change theirs. The more willing I am to build a better me, the easier it is for others to work on themselves.

What do I need to change?

What are my blind spots?

How do I discover them?

This book will offer opportunities for you to discover uniqueness in you. It will open limitless possibilities to see yourself differently by giving you new viewpoints to change yourself and start building a better you. It will improve the quality of your life and your relationships. It will change your haphazard approach to relationships to a strategic and intentional approach impacting who you are and how you show up.

Let's get started.

Anxiety vs. Intellect

What's the big deal?

A couple in Texas made the news in July 2002[1] when a wife ran over her cheating husband. This happened at a hotel where he and his lover were exiting after a rendezvous. The wife, knowing they were at the hotel, positioned herself in the parking lot. When they exited the hotel, she ran over him three times in her car.

This is an extreme example of operating at high anxiety and making a choice that caused multiple tragedies, a death, a prison term, the children's loss of both parents, financial ruin, and horrible anguish for family and friends.

She was convicted of murder and served 15 years of a 20-year sentence. She and her husband had a successful dental practice together. Being a highly educated dentist did not stop her from making a very irrational decision out of anxiety that cost the family severely. This does not minimize his awful mistakes. She was hurt horribly and acted out of extreme anxiety and emotional pain. [BLIND SPOT]

This kind of reaction out of high anxiety makes my point. *I have found in myself and others that acting more emotional than intellect/spirituality during the height of anxiety causes regretful actions and decisions.*

Anxiety and intellect compete for the same available brain resources.

● Diagram 1—**Anxiety Up | Intellect Down**
  As anxiety is up and intellect goes down.

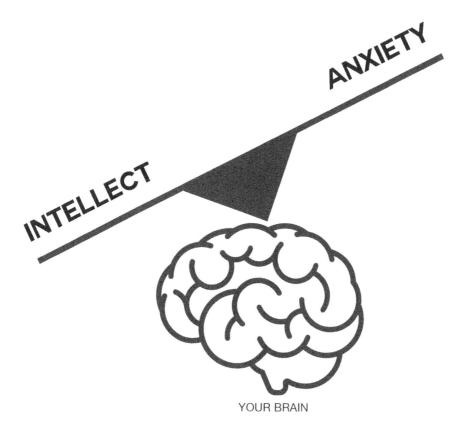

YOUR BRAIN

The more anxious I am the less intellectual. The more intellectual I am the less anxious. I view anxiety and intellect as inversely proportionate. When one goes up, the other goes down. See examples provided.

The key to this concept is knowing when anxiety has overridden my intellect.

● Diagram 2—**Intellect Up | Anxiety Down**

As intellect is up and anxiety goes down.

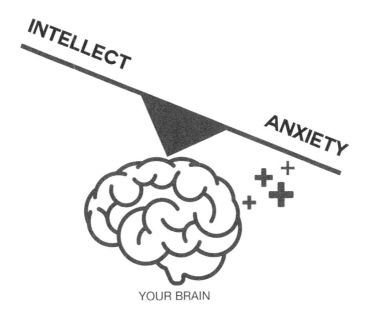

YOUR BRAIN

● Diagram 3—**Intellect = Anxiety Equal**

When anxiety and intellect are relatively equal, great choices are available.

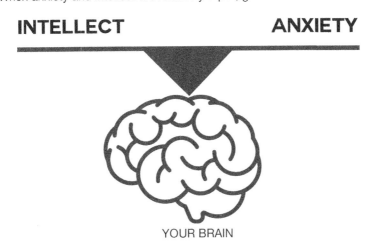

YOUR BRAIN

We are in peak performance to make the best, healthiest, most productive choices when the intellect is equal to our emotions.

Example: I have heard this wife's story many times...after a terrible argument where injurious words were spoken to her and a short time later the husband asks, *"Why don't we go have sex?"* She says, *"Are you kidding me, after all you said and did?"* He let out his aggression—anxiety up, intellect down—dumping it on her and expected things to be alright.

I recently talked to another woman who told of her husband getting extremely angry at her, venting his wrath on her. She was awestruck and did not know how to respond. She distanced herself so that she could feel safe. I just received a text from her, as I am writing this—she said, *"Now he is asking me out tonight for drinks."* **Fascinating!**
[BIG BLIND SPOT]

Other examples would be angry spouses, angry parents, road rage, out of control individuals who are hurting and choose to afflict others either physically, or emotionally. My belief is that they feel completely justified in the moment, only to have second thoughts later.

As you saw in the examples, when intellect/spirituality and anxiety are equal, a resonance is created that allows a balance of cognition and emotions.

During this phenomenon, our passion is fueled by our intellect, and it is at this instant that we can be most creative, ingenious, and become a masterful problem solver. Operating within this balance enables us to master our skills in decision making. What an opportunity to build, support, or recreate something new.

This revelation opened a wonderful opportunity for me to recognize that going out of control to gain control, initiated operating in an anxious mode. The more anxious I become, the more I say and do the things I inevitably regret. I think about people who hurt other people physically, maybe even assault or murder. They are totally behaving out of high anxiety without any intellect involved.

So how do I know that I am in an anxious mode?

For me, I experience an increased heart rate, my thinking gets rapid, the amplitude of my voice gets elevated and at times I stand, my fist might clench, or many other physiological changes will occur. This is where self-control must come into play.

Decisions made from high anxiety are usually not intellectual, as demonstrated in the examples provided. Perhaps you have experienced this also.

> We are in peak performance to make the best, healthiest, most productive choices when the intellect is equal to our emotions.

Going out of control to gain control

(The Oxymoron)

It comes back again to self-control and being able to identify what is going on with my body, and mind. When I recognize I am in an anxious mode, I do any and everything I can to ensure that I am not engaging with someone in a manner that is out of anger or any anxious emotions. I must employ any intellectual abilities I can muster. This helps me become more in control of myself, thus being able to deescalate a potential hazardous conversation or situation.

> ## I sometimes say God did not give me a *"check engine"* light.

If I did have a check engine light that showed my anxiety is overriding my intellect, it would be easy for me to recognize, disengage, and to be sure that I do not cause more damage to myself, the other person, or the relationship.

Acting out of my anxiety is what I call "going out of control to gain control."

When I feel stressed or attacked, it brings rise for me to need to get bigger and louder. Going out of control to gain control takes me out of the logical, rational part of my brain. It ensures I will become much less emotionally mature and feel I must resort to survival mode.

When I recognize any of these "check engine light" symptoms, I know immediately my way of getting back in control is to sit down or in some way physically lower my eye level to the one I am speaking. When I subordinate myself to the other person,

I gain control of myself rather than go out of control. I notice when subordinating myself, the amplitude of my voice becomes much lower and the context of my communication becomes much more congenial and connected. The more intellectual I present, the better the outcome of the communication.

Note to self: *Of course, do not do this if you are driving or in any other compromising situation.*

To avoid going out of control to gain control, I become self-conscious and look at my reaction to the circumstances. When my boys were young, even through their teenage years, our disagreements became confrontational and the more confrontational they became, the worse the situation was intensified. The more the situation grew out of control, the more controlling I would behave. [BLIND SPOT]

Going out of control to gain control? It makes no sense, yet I used to be masterful at it. I thought I was gaining control. I leaned forward, perhaps my hands on my hips, a very loud voice and sometimes even spitting as I forced words out. My face was distorted. Self-control was nonexistent.

I can see now, all I was doing was subduing, hurting, or shutting down the other person. Perhaps even breaking their spirit. *OUCH!* This had to make them feel like they had no voice, no sense of connection or understanding from me. This spilled over into my relationship with my wife. I had to win and thus they got to lose. How embarrassing.

What a difficult situation to be in when talking to the ones I love the most. I shut them down and pushed them away instead of attracting them to me so I could give them the kind of love, coaching and self-confidence they needed and deserved.

Spilled milk…the next 10 seconds he will remember for a lifetime.

Let us look at a situation where my 5-year-old son was being overly active at the breakfast table. There was great laughter and an interchange of fun conversation. Suddenly he accidentally knocks over a glass of milk.

In the next 10 seconds, will I be mindful of and acknowledge that it was not done in malice?

How will he feel about himself when this accident is cleaned up?

How will he feel about me?

Regardless of how I act, in the next 10 seconds, he will remember this moment for a lifetime. It is my belief that he would already be in pain, and regret doing anything that upsets us, as his parents. Often, I ask children what it is like when they do anything that upsets their parents. Generally, the answer is *"I do not like it."* But I as a parent did not process the situation that way.

It is easy for me to feel like I must express my discontent with harsh correction, not thinking about what their experience of the situation might be. That does not mean they get away with anything they do intentionally wrong. It just means it is important for me to consider their experience. Looking at the emotional side of relationships can bring familial health.

What is my intention?

The milk spilled, and no one can go back and unring this bell.

Nothing can change the circumstance, so do I use this as a learning opportunity to grow, teach, reinforce, and correct in such a way that he can learn from it and do so with confidence?

The glass of milk spilled: what is going to be his lasting memory?

Here is a real-life circumstance where I get to make a defining choice, and I will choose based on my ability to apply self-control. If I am stressed, hurt, worried, frustrated, or anxious in any way, I might respond by going out of control to gain control. If I am in my rational, logical, reasonable mind, then my method of handling this situation will be much different.

If I am emotionally elevated, I might say or ask things like... (expletive delete)

"Look what you have done?"

"Why don't you pay attention?"

"How many times have I told you not to play at the table?"

"You are always doing something careless like this?"

These kinds of responses are examples of breaking the child's spirit, causing them to feel bad about themselves and what they have done. A broken spirit leads to a lack of confidence. Lack of confidence leads to the inability to connect in healthy ways in their social environment. It is damaging to their emotional maturity. It can begin a pattern of lifelong, automatic, negative self-talk. This pervasive display of emotion can be damaging to them for a lifetime.

Young minds are precious and most desire to be recognized as pleasing young individuals who want love and attention from their parents. If one of my boys made a mistake when I was filled with anxiety, too many times I overreacted and went out of control to gain control. It was easy for me to understand and appreciate the cause of my overreaction, but the recipient of the guff, discipline, or punishment had no clue what is going on within me. They felt the pain of being wrong, rejected, yelled at, diminished, or even cut from the herd. Perhaps they were even told to get away from the table.

The pain has been administered. Disappointing the parent has been felt, it is seared in the mind and sometimes used as self-admonishment to indicate unworthiness or prove to themselves that they are bad and wrong when they make mistakes. It can be their proof that they do a lot of things to dissatisfy their parents and perhaps others.

Now let us look at an example of self-control. Acting out of intellect as opposed to anxious emotions.

What is it we want them to learn?

Are they bad?

Are they only mistake ridden or loved and in a learning process?

What do we want them to say about themselves when the situation is over?

What do we want them to say about us when that situation is over?

What do we want to say about ourselves under these conditions?

How easy is it to bolster a child's spirit; help them feel their worthiness and cause them to have the self-confidence they so deserve? By no means am I saying that mistakes do not need to be rectified. Carelessness needs to be identified and corrected.

I look at young children as fragile but resilient. As I mentioned earlier, most children will say, without even thinking, they dislike disappointing their parents. Some say they hate it! More say it makes them feel bad. Others are harder on themselves, with automatic negative self-talk, than their parents could be.

Another approach to dealing with the "spilled milk" scenario, would be asking the child if they are OK. I might ask them to help me clean it up, and while we are cleaning up, ask them what they learned. In this story, I get to tell them how smart they are and compliment them as opposed to degrading them. I could ask them if they see what they did and how it initiated a chain of events that were not so positive. I would reassure them that they are a great person, and I am glad they learned something about growing up and knowing when we make a mistake. We can learn to be aware the next time, so it does not happen again.

> ### Finding connection with God can help us gain self-composure.

As children turn to adolescents and young adults get older, sometimes their mistakes may be more severe and require a different way of teaching and molding. Using this model of being in control of myself will help me teach and mold confidence rather than utilizing punishment thus breaking their spirit.

So how will he feel when this spilled milk situation ends? It will depend on how I express my feelings toward him. How he feels about me will determine what he experiences during this event. If I want him saying good things about me and himself, I must be intentional and strategic about not going out of control to gain control.

> **Paying attention to my emotions,**
> **allows me to be in control of my choices**
> **and enables me to build a better me.**

When we are small, we learn to manage chaos, conflict, or stress by having temper tantrums, avoiding, filibustering, placating, using humor, and many other tactics that are a result of choices we make when under stress. This conclusion is based solely on my study and observations of human behavior. It seems to me that we carry these same approaches of dealing with stress into our adult life—handling stress and conflict in a very adolescent and immature and ineffective manner.

Having a temper tantrum in adult life to solve a disagreement may temporarily cause the one having the tantrum to feel like he has won, or the situation has been resolved. This choice only worsens the chaotic state of affairs. This is just another example of going out of control to gain control. [BLIND SPOT]

I propose the conflict or disagreement has only been put on hold to surface later when stress or chaos resurfaces. I subscribe to the idea of using intellect/spirituality, coupled with empathy, to resolve conflict or disagreement in relationships.

Understanding the other person's point of view or asking gently curious questions allows them to state their cause, results in reducing stress and tension through consideration and sensitivity.

Can I make it about understanding and appreciation as opposed to being right and winning?

Can I look to the future to see what the overall outcome could be instead of looking at the petty details to win an argument or try to convince them?

What results do I want to attain?

Respond in a manner that creates beneficial outcomes for both as opposed to just winning the argument.

Here are four ways I see to develop and mature in life; physical, intellectual, spiritual, and emotional growth.

Physical growth occurs through eating, drinking, exercising, and sleeping.

Intellectual growth occurs by attending school, studying, and learning through life's lessons.

Spiritual growth occurs through reading, study, worship, and association with others of like belief.

Emotional growth occurs through diligent study of emotions and how to recognize them. This can be a lengthy process. Being capable of identifying my own emotions and the emotions of others gives me the ability to make healthy choices. I am equipped to stay emotionally healthy and manage myself regardless of the circumstances.

When I am under duress, I need to pause, ask myself to place an age on my behavior, my choice of words, and my physical reaction. Under duress of my past, I would say I acted the age of a child or a young adolescent. If I choose a respected friend and ask myself how he might handle this conflicting situation, then choose their method, I will come out of the conflict in charge of myself. This kind of self-management will give me the opportunity to defuse rather than escalate a situation. This is a skillful way of changing myself when in chaos. Regardless of what the circumstances are, my reaction to them will determine the outcome of the situation. I have authority to influence the outcome I desire.

> ## By changing myself, I can influence change in others.

Without thinking, I can damage relationships by saying or doing things I will regret later. The more anxious I become, the more serious my actions are and that is how mishaps happen. This is where irrevocable mistakes are made that may be irreparable to relationships, jobs, and other pivotal areas in my life.

So, what do I do with this?

The instant I find myself getting anxious, the first thing I want to do is seek self-control; otherwise, I will go out of control to gain control. Self-control, for me, begins with subordinating myself to the other person. I will not do this if I sense danger to myself. If danger seems evident, I will leave the situation. In the proper circumstance, subordinating myself means dropping my eye level below theirs. If they are standing, I might sit. If they are sitting, I might sit on the floor. With a physiological shift comes an emotional shift. My voice will become calmer, the contents of my communication shifts to perceiving and listening. I completely disengage my reptilian brain. *I have seen this happen many times and have employed it myself. It works for me.*

I don't know if you have ever gone out of control to gain control. I have many times and didn't know it. My intentions had to do with controlling others or a situation in which I had no control. *The only thing I had control of was me...which was foreign to me at the time.*

In the TV series, *Funniest Home Videos*, I am reminded of the man who is trying to start his weed eater. After pulling the rope multiple times and it not starting, he began to bang the weed eater on the concrete, then turning it around, began to hit the non-compliant engine as hard as he could, bending and breaking every piece. He then threw it down and stomped away. This is a good example of going out of control to gain control. I don't know if any of you have ever done that, or perhaps you might know someone who has? How embarrassing, *especially if the neighbors are watching.* [BLIND SPOT]

The catalyst of these out-of-control emotions is usually unclear and is not in my conscious mind. If I am calm, strategic, and intentional about starting the weed eater, I will pursue other methods of solving the problem. I will not choose anger and destruction.

If I am very uptight, worried about finances, relationships, work, or children, rather than destroy the weed eater, I need to get myself under control by identifying and reducing the major stressors in my life. This is where I see resentments and frustrations accumulate to build a powerful invisible bomb that can and will explode at inopportune times. [See Global Thinking page 64]

These stressors play out in ways that do not fit the circumstances. *I call it giving two dollars' worth of guff for a nickel's worth of offense.*

Often blind spots are so far buried from my awareness that I am clueless as to how they are impacting my current actions. Circumstances that I was not aware of and situations I had masked over the past are great influencer's on my daily choices. The more hidden the blind spots, the more I said and did things that I felt remorse about later. This is yet another case of going out of control to gain control—*anxiety overriding my intellect/spirituality.*

I was talking to a man who was having trouble with his girl-friend because she was talking to another man. He called her terrible names and told her she was dead to him. Later when he was not so angry and feeling better, he contacted her to tell her that he was so sorry. She replied, *"Yes you are and now that I know who you are, I do not want to have a relationship with you."* This is a case in point of allowing emotions to override intellect/spirituality and losing something very important in life.

Resist the oxymoron, seek self-control!

My Reptilian Brain

Fight, Flight or Freeze

In the previous example of spilled milk, I would certainly say that going out of control to gain control is me operating from my 'reptilian brain' as opposed to from the rational brain or the portion of the brain that responds to situations with rational and logical responses that lead to good judgment.

My definition of the reptilian brain is that portion of the brain that takes care of all the vital body functioning, such as heart rate, respiration, body temperature, digestion, and the rest of the automatic and involuntary body functions. It also oversees the fight, flight, or freeze actions that take place unconsciously. There have been too many times that I have made choices acting out of my reptilian brain.

Have you ever heard of this term, *'reptilian brain'* regarding relationships?

I found I used this part of my brain when I could not get someone to do what I thought they needed to be doing or get them to see the things from my point of view. This is where I found myself going into "convince" or "prove it" mode.

This portion of my brain renders me uncontrollable, unruly, ungovernable, insubordinate, and defiant.

It did not seem like I was going out of control. It seemed natural that if my being right was in question, I was not about to allow this to take place. I allowed my voice to escalate in amplitude and harshness, I positioned my body to show I am the aggressor and operated out of my reptilian brain—these were total blind spots for me.

Observing small species of animals all the way up to watching elephants posture themselves as they are frightened or upset, is somewhat the same with me, I get loud, stand up, present myself as powerfully as I can.

As mentioned, my reptilian brain function consists of fight, flight or freeze and whenever confronted, I was conditioned to resort to fight. If someone would have told me that I was out of control under those circumstances, I would probably have gotten angry with them and argued that was not the case. If you did not respond to my satisfaction, I would act as though you did not hear me and repeat the same thing even louder. How intellectual is that? [BLIND SPOT]

If you were to try to convince me, my behavior at that time would not get the results I was looking for, I would have let you know, in no uncertain terms, you were wrong. My reptilian brain can get in the way of finding a balanced perspective, practicing compassion, and pursuing happiness.

Ultimately, the choice is up to me, and what I choose goes a long way to determine who I become and the direction my life will take—both in a practical sense of achieving greater success, and in a spiritual sense of becoming a loving and kind human being.

> **I have to learn to stop, focus, respond in my intellect/spirituality and not act out of my reptilian brain to foster emotionally healthy relationships.**

Reptilian Brain Function

The fight, flight, or freeze response is the body's built-in response mechanism whenever anxiety-provoking situations present themselves.

FIGHT
Engage

RESPONSE: Attack, Confront, Dominate

EMOTION: Anger, Irritable

OUTCOME: Insult, Blame, Mistreat

FLIGHT
Escape

RESPONSE: Run, Hide, Quit

EMOTION: Denial, Anxious

OUTCOME: Evade, Omit, Sabotage

FREEZE
Disengage

RESPONSE: Comply, Surrender

EMOTION: Shutdown, Empty, Numb

OUTCOME: Justify, Rationalize, Detach

Safe Listening

Those who have ears to hear, let them hear...

Many years ago, I was talking with a mom who told me she had a 15-year-old daughter. Her daughter told her everything. She knew who was having sex, who was sneaking out at night, who was cheating on their exams, who was doing alcohol and drugs. She knew about her daughter's friends' families and some of their problems. She said, *"I do not know what to do with all this information."* I said, *"Ma'am, whatever you are doing, keep it up. You want her coming to you with all of this information so she can hear from you how she should handle these situations and not go to her friends or others who might steer her in a direction unacceptable to you."*

I began to think of myself when I was a young father, and how I was not a good nor a safe listener. If my son would have told me one of his friends was smoking cigarettes, I would have probably, in a very stern tone, let him know immediately I better not catch him smoking cigarettes or even having a lighter or matches. This would have hindered any opportunity for my son to ever come to me and tell me anything. He had received my autocratic wrath; he was in trouble based on what his friend was doing.

> **I thought I was saying the right things.**
> **But it only repelled him.**

It caused him to not want to share information with me because of my judgmental attitude. My inability to hear his story and act on that information with good judgment was completely thrown out the door.

Why would he ever tell me anything again? I did not provide a safe listening place for him to share.

Are you too quick to give advice? If you are, you tell the other person what they need to do before they even ask.

If you interrupt, you are telling others that they need to be quiet and listen to you because what you say is more important.

I can assess myself to see if I am a safe listener or not. Look at the questions below and answer them for yourself before you proceed with the rest of this section. Think about your relationship with your children, spouse, neighbors, friends, family, or coworkers and see how you measure up. It is interesting to compare how I assess myself on these questions and how others assess me if they are allowed to be completely candid.

When talking to others, would others say you are a safe Listener?

- *Do you interrupt?*
- *Are you too quick to give advice?*
- *Do you cut the speaker off in some way?*
- *Do you tell hero stories?*
- *Do they feel important when speaking to you?*
- *Are they afraid or intimidated by you?*
- *Do they feel safe to disagree?*
- *Is their voice important?*
- *Do you talk more than you listen?*
- *Do you not talk enough?*
- *Do you embarrass them in any way?*

These questions are relationship changers if I will choose to use them for my advantage. Safe listening involves self-control. Not allowing my emotions to override my intellect/spirituality, but being strategic and intentional about the way I process what I am hearing. This ensures that I am considering everything that is going on with myself and the speaker and connecting with them in a way that makes a difference for them.

The more I allow people to talk, the more they hear their own voice and can talk themselves off the ledge or feel great about the connecting conversation they are having with me.

COMMUNICATION
is the key to successful relationships.

SAFE LISTENING
is the key to successful communication.

YO! LISTEN TO UNDERSTAND, NOT REPLY.

Gently curious questions

What stories are you telling yourself?

Combined with safe listening are 'gently curious' questions. 'Gently curious' questions softly probe the thoughts and ideas of a person in a way that causes them to learn more about themselves. It allows them to drill down and get to the deeper meaning to the circumstances that may be contributing to their problems or conditions.

Gently curious questions lightly examine the thoughts and ideas of another person in a way that causes them to learn more about themselves. It also gives the inquirer important knowledge about them.

If I want to connect, I must engage with their emotional state and talk about things that are related to their thoughts and emotions. I also need to pay attention to what is going on with me. If their emotional state makes me emotional, I may want to help override their emotions by fixing or offering suggestions to get them out of that emotional state. [BLIND SPOT] Now I am making this about me instead of them.

Look at these gently curious questions and utilize them as a guide for your future conversations.

Using gently curious questions:

- *Help me understand?*
- *What else can you tell me about this?*
- *What do you need from me?*
- *I'm confused, can you elaborate?*

- *What is not being said that needs to be said?*
- *Create your own Gently Curious Questions.*

Each answer to a gently curious question can be the source of the next question.

'Why' is not a gently curious question. It is caustic. It says, *'Prove to me and I bet you can't.'* [See *'Why'* in Relationships starting page 122]

Example: Suppose a good friend tells me their dog is sick and may have to be put to sleep. I can join with them empathetically and ask questions like:

"How long have you had your dog?"

"What is your dog's name?"

"What do you like about this dog?"

"How does this dog compare to any other pets you have had?"

The more we talk about these generalities' pertaining to their dog, the more the other person realizes the importance, significance, and role this animal plays in their life. It may cause them to feel more sadness which is completely appropriate due to the love, memories, and fear of loss, which if not handled in an effective manner, only produces more misery. The sadness is there because of the connection they have had with the animal. These gently curious questions help them continue to express the grief side of loss. All of these kinds of questions are asked in the gentlest manner. If the person becomes the least bit upset, I will back down immediately. I just want to assist them in processing not causing extra grief. This is a delicate process.

If I just say, *"That is terrible,"* or *"You will get over it,"* *"You will get another pet,"* or *"Let me tell you about the one I lost."* I have insulted them as opposed to making a connection with them.

> **This kind of insight and connection includes recognizing their issue and being able to empathize and not fix.**

Too many times fixing is the intent when I see someone suffering, especially someone I love or who is important to me. When they suffer, I suffer and to relieve my suffering, I want to make them feel better. My attempt to make them feel better may actually make them feel worse.

Before I was a counselor, if my son had come to me and said, *"I'm not handsome or I'm not smart,"* the first thing I would reply is *"Oh yes you are! You're the smartest young man I know,"* or *"You're very bright"* or, *"You're very handsome."*

Believe it or not this will only confound the issue. When someone says they are not smart, pretty, or handsome, it is because in their mind; they are very confused, frustrated, or have logical examples that back up their statement. Coming to me in this state of frustration and confusion and me countering their thinking, I am telling them they are wrong. This is not helpful and adds to their confusion. Until I can help them recognize and reduce the cause of their emotions, I cannot help them reduce their stress and they will stay in a confused state. After answering all the gently curious questions, they can then collect the thoughts ricocheting in their head. Allow them time to clearly explain and make sense of their thinking.

My desire to fix is an interesting phenomenon and a common trap that I suggest we can all fall into. It is not, however, one that is helpful for the person who has expressed their issue with us. They are not wanting to be changed. They are expressing their frustration and confusion. They are reaching out for connection. I had always assumed they needed to be fixed. Not so, they are wanting to be heard, not wanting to be told what to do. ***They are needing to hear their own voice.***

'Gently Curious' questions need to be accepted, not challenged or discounted.

As they answer these questions, whatever they say is okay. Remember, they are attempting to reduce stress by talking it out. This is not a time to debate their feelings but to encourage them in exploring their feelings through questions.

Your stance is to support them by assisting them to drill down and identify as much as they can about what they are experiencing. This is a great way of assisting them to move forward and make the most difference in their situation.

Use their answers to identify more gently curious questions.

Anytime they offer an answer make a question from it. This helps guide them to grasp and perhaps comprehend what they are truly facing. Anytime you ask these questions, I encourage you to stay on the curious side not the fixing side.

After the conversation has ended, I suggest you wait a minimum of two hours, then go to them and make a statement such as, "remember when you said you were not handsome, would it be okay if I did not agree with that?"

Letting time pass fosters connection, and now the compliment can be heard and will very likely dispel some of the struggles uncovered earlier.

The low hanging fruit has to do with the first part, being gently curious, allowing them to speak, exhausting the stress that is instigating their strife, struggle, and strain.

Gently curious questions emerge from the content of the conversation.

Remember, when a person makes a statement such as **"I am sad,"** it is important to take in consideration any descriptive word, any adjective describing them, is on a continuum of mild to chronic. It is essential to determine where on that continuum they are speaking from. Otherwise, we may be misinterpreting their level of sadness. They can be mildly sad, perhaps debilitated, or anywhere in between. Take a look at the pain scale.

PAIN SCALE CONTINUUM

Adjectives used to describe us are on a continuum. For example, **'sad'** can be mild or chronic or anywhere in between.

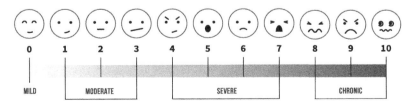

Gentle questions will assist them in enlightening me of where they are on the continuum. I don't want the ones that I love to be sad, in a negative mood or emotional. It is often fun and beneficial to bring something to the table which causes their mood to shift. I like to see them in a good place and asking gently curious questions draws this out of them.

If I am fused with their mood and they are sad, mad, angry, or hurt, then it is easy to follow suit. I need to remain in my mood, invite them out of the dark—in a very kind and unassuming way—into the light.

Another avenue of using gently curious questions is to ask the question, so that the person answering, tells you, what you want to tell them. Read that again. *Ask the question, so that the person answering, tells you, what you want to tell them.* If Joey leaves his backpack on the kitchen floor, I might ask, *"Joey, what do you think I will ask you to do with your backpack?"* He might grumble and say, *"You want me to put it in my room."* This is opportunity for me to catch him doing things right and well. Now I get to say, *"Joey, I love it when you know what I need from you. You are the best kid in town."*

An anxious mind cannot hear facts

I have to remind myself; **safe listening, 'gently curious' questions and time, allow me to learn more about myself and others.** It is knowledge I do not obtain if I am always trying to fix people.

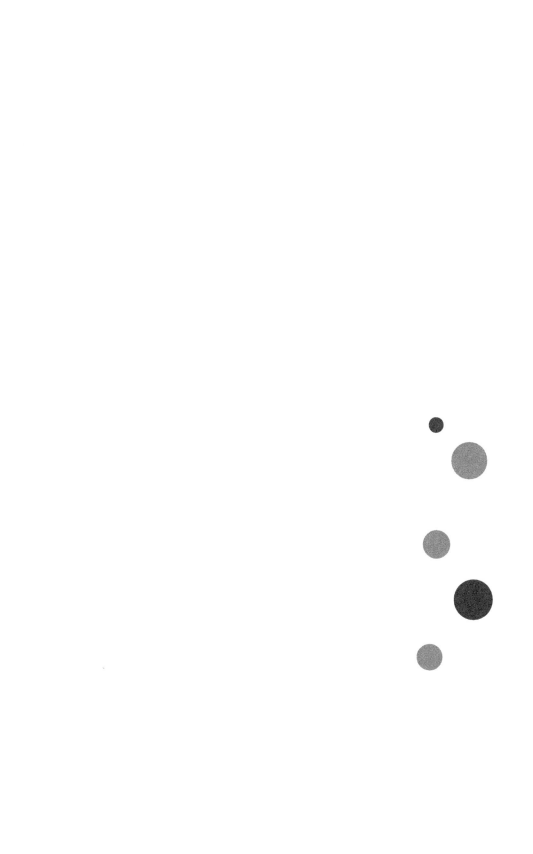

Clear, Consistent, Do not Convince

Who is in charge here?

Being clear and consistent is powerful in relationships.

If I must convince someone about who I am or what I need, I find myself in an unhealthy conversation. The more I know myself, and all that is going on with me, the more I can master my situation. Staying out of convincing another person that I'm right and they are wrong is crucial.

There is nothing wrong with having two opinions. It is alright if my opinion is not being accepted by someone else.

When I am truly in charge of myself, it does not matter.

I can get through it by maintaining a great sense of self control. I call this being *'clear, consistent and do not convince.'* When I am clear about who I am, where I am going and I am consistent, I do not need to convince anyone of anything. I can allow myself to have a point of view and accept others' points of view without creating chaos or argument. Arguments are a result of each attempting to convince the other. Arguments are not bad unless they become destructive to the relationship.

When I am clear about who I am, where I am going, and act the same every day, I do not need to convince anyone of anything. I may not get my way, but at least I do not have to do anything that could damage the relationship.

Example: Putting children to bed. When I am in convince mode, I spend evening after evening negotiating, chasing them down, getting drinks of water before they will get into bed. If I am not clear and consistent from the beginning, it causes a problem for both of us.

If they refuse my request, I encourage them to choose wisely knowing there will be consequences if they do not. Consequences could be going to bed earlier the next night or losing a privilege of their choice.

Who is in charge here?

If the rules for my request are not followed, and they ask the next day if they could have permission to do something, I would remind them of the night before, asking them the gently curious question, *"Based on how you disrespected my request last night, do you think I should allow you to do that?"* Be clear, be consistent.

Isn't it true that kids are fascinated by asking questions? Questions about everything.

"How come clouds float?"

"How come the sky is blue?"

"What makes cars go?"

As parents, we are focused on their intent to learn. It is easy for us to do whatever we need to, to teach and explain the answers. However, when questions become stumbling blocks, such as, *"Why do I have to go to bed now?"* The more I try to convince the more frustrating things become.

Anytime I start to convince, I lose control. I go into *"convince mode"* and go out of control to gain control, getting angry, saying, and doing things I might regret. Losing control to the *"convincing game"* only incites vexation and the less sense it makes.

Gently curious questions shift the listener's role. Rather than you trying to convince, they will sort through their answer to their feelings on the matter. And this increases willingness and acceptance to do what is being asked. The answer to the question isn't just any answer; it's their answer, reflecting their own personal thoughts, beliefs, and preferences. That makes it more likely to drive action.

> **Say it to yourself,**
> **"When I am clear, I do not need to convince."**

Now my actions and behaviors are my convincing tools. The more in control I stay, the less I want to control others. The more adequately I contribute to the conversation and reduce anxiety, the more intellect, care, and love are allowed to take effect. *When I am confident, clear, and consistent, I show I care by being an example of self-control and emotional maturity.*

Global Thinking
Causing your own distress

Global thinking refers to identifying life's issues that key up anxiety, stress and worry.

Examples: Illness, money, job, relationships, children, automobiles, house, and many other stressors are each unique to my circumstances.

When I cannot see beyond today's stressors, I draw them on a large sheet of paper. At first my mind might be focused on relationships, then it bounces down to children, then to illness, money, house, job, then back to illness. From illness it goes to job, car, children, house then back to money. From money to illness, job, relationship and back to children. From children, to relationships, car, and back to house. I begin to see how my mind pings and bounces from one worry or stressor to the next and then back again over and over and over.

All this bouncing produces nothing, but more worry and time squandered. As you can see in diagram, S1 page 66. I can spend as much time as I choose bouncing back and forth and not getting anything resolved. It consumes an extraordinary amount of energy for little to no healthy results. ***What a waste!*** Before I resolve anything pertaining to money, I have jumped to the next stressor and on to the next. I can now see that chaos is in control of my thinking thus producing major anxiety.

As I allow these thoughts to ping and bounce, nothing gets settled. I make up a ***worry story*** which is negative and clouds my thinking even more. I am not doing anything to relieve my thinking or stressors. My worry story is producing more stress, and my desire for a sense of calmness does not have a chance. I am off again on another thought ricocheting and bouncing around until I wear myself out and become frustrated, confused, and more anxious.

I may look for an undesirable means of finding relief. This is where

● Diagram S1—**Stessors Worry Story**

My worry story is producing more stress and my desire for a sense of calmness does not have a chance.

today's stressors

relationships

illness

children

car

house

money

job

alcohol, drugs, gambling, arguing, and many other anesthetizing habits become employed. [BLIND SPOT]

In my experience, I have seen what people face moment by moment, day by day, year after year—bouts with chronic illness, being the child of abuse, losing a business, changing careers—all these are just small samplings that are causing anxiety to rise. Anxiety propels me into the future, pulling me from the present, and leading me into my reptilian brain producing fight, flight, or freeze.

Cognition is no longer present. I must disengage my inner bully; stop, focus, and get control of myself—intellect/spirituality up, anxiety down. Being aware that my thinking influences my distress can be very freeing and extinguish anxiety before it gets a hold on my emotions.

Global thinking is a wicked paradox.

Four questions to pursue pertaining to each stressor when dealing with global thinking:

"What I know?"

"What do I not know?"

"What can I do?"

"What I cannot do about this subject?"

If I look at the stressor of 'job' mentioned in the figure on the left, and apply these four questions, it opens possibilities that I have not been considering.

What I know: (about my job)

I have been here 5 years - I like some of my co-workers - It is extremely stressful - I feel underpaid - Others are paid more - It has a short commute - I am overqualified - Denied a pay increase - My boss is a jerk - I had planned to only be here 3 years - I do not feel supported at home - I have too much overtime - I feel unappreciated - I really want something different - I want a better salary - I am not excited to go to work

What I do not know: (about my job)

If I can find a better one - If I would be satisfied - If there would be cliques there - If I would feel challenged - If a change would be satisfying for me - If I would get the support at home - If I could find something close to home - If I could make more money

What can I do? (about my job)

Give up thinking about it - accept my plight - Dust off my resume - Network with friends - Get serious about looking - Begin a search process - See if there are headhunters in my profession - Get a positive attitude - Sign on my spouse for support - Set some small, timed sensitive goals - Not give up

What can I not do? (about my job)

Change the people - Get a different boss - Get more money - Know if a change would make me happy

From this I have concluded that I will look at what I can do to seriously begin a job search. I will not know what is available until I get committed to looking at all my options. This helps me feel unstuck and like I have a direction.

If through this exercise, I concluded to stay, I will come up with a plan to make the best of what I have and definitely not complain to myself about it. When my thinking pings to the stressor, job, now I can feel comfort in my new plan.

When I take each worry or stressor through this exercise, peace and comfort begin to replace stress and anxiety. The more I write about each question, the better this process works. I get a better sense of what I can do when each appears in my thinking. Knowing I have processed each one of them can produce a wonderful sense of calm. This exercise can be used for any stressor.

Get your free downloadable Global Thinking Worry/Stressor Worksheet at www.jerrydclark.com/globalthinking

RMJ

The Filibuster Fantasy

Have you ever found yourself justifying your behavior, then ratio-nalizing it, only to justify it further to minimize your actions, so you can blame, redirect, or deflect? Have you ever been on the receiving end of this behavior?

People who rationalize, minimize, and justify are frustrating to attempt to communicate with and do not realize it. I see them as a slippery fish, wiggling, struggling, jerking, trying to get away without connecting. They can come across as self-righteous and terribly unattractive without knowing it. They have pushed people away and are totally unaware. I do not see this done in malevolence but with the thought of preserving an image, utilizing an excessive use of words to deflect meaning or place decoys that draw the focus from a perceived accusation. Take a look at what *Webster*[2] has to say about each word so we are on the same page as we discuss RMJ further.

Rationalize is a *"way of describing, interpreting, or explaining something (such as bad behavior) that makes it seem proper, more attractive, etc."*

Minimize is a *"way of reducing or keeping to a minimum, to underes-timate intentionally, to put down, diminish, depreciate, belittle, etc."*

Justify is a *"way to provide a good reason for qualifying, asserting, defending, upholding their truth as authentic in order to look good in the face of a challenge."*

Example: Jeff and Suzanne have been married for 10 years. They have two children, five and eight. The relationship has its ups but mostly downs. Suzanne seems to be pulling away emotionally and communicatively. She is not feeling as close as she once did. Suzanne makes requests of Jeff but gets frustrated due to feeling unheard and undervalued.

Here is a typical conversation:

Suzanne: *"You don't hear me."*

Jeff: *"Yes I do. I hear you fine. I hear every word you say."*

Suzanne: *"I just don't think you do."*

Jeff: *"I always listen to you. Perhaps you don't give me credit for anything."*

Suzanne: *"This is what I'm talking about. Regardless of what I say you explain it away and I just feel unheard, empty, and foolish for even saying what I want from you."*

Jeff: *"I am a good husband and provider. I don't know why you can't see the good things about me."*

Suzanne: *"Forget it."* She pulls back further.

Emotional closeness and communication are fractured.

This kind of poor communications leaves both parties exasperated and distant. As this continues, Suzanne will pull back silently and resentfully. Unless these resentments go away, or things change considerably, this relationship can easily result in a breakup. This would totally blindside Jeff because he is not aware of his contribution to the relationship that is embittering Suzanne. Under these circumstances, Jeff will be completely surprised and may even ask the question, *"Why didn't you tell me?"* [BLIND SPOT]

The fascinating truth in this conversation is that if Jeff could have connected with her in attempting to understand and appreciate her sentiment of wanting him to engage with her, he could have been the hero, not the goat.

Jeff could have asked gently curious questions to help alleviate the confusion:

"Help me understand."

"Tell me what I do that causes you to feel that way."

"Give me just a few examples. I think it will help me."

"Will you point it out the next time you experience me doing this?"

Another example of RMJ would be when the wife says to the husband, *"You left a glass in the sink,"* in which he quickly retorts, *"You left a pan on the stove."* Wife then replies, *"Why do you always turn it around on me?"* Husband says, *"I'm not turning it around on you, I'm just stating a fact like you did."* With exasperation the wife says, *"I don't know why you don't just accept what I say rather than turn it around on me."* Husband growls, *"You stated a fact; I did the same."*

This is a classic example of not accepting what was being said and wanting to rationalize, minimize, or justify a situation. Also, there is unfinished business on his part in the conversation. If he wanted the pan removed from the stove, he should have mentioned it earlier.

It is easy to see this in slow motion; it's difficult in the moment.

This conversation could have been interpreted that he did not want to look bad in his wife's eyes, and his immediate reaction caused him to go in defense mode. The frustrating fact is, in her eyes, it made him look awful anyway. We do not know of the stress level of either party here. If high stress is present, it could be significant.

Here are a few examples of how each could have handled this circumstance differently:

If he would have acquiesced and put the glass away and told her she was right, it would make him look like a hero to her.

If she had removed the glass and mentioned to him that she did and reminded him to please not do that the next time, it could have softened the conversation.

If either could have recognized their emotions were high, they could have had some great conversation pertaining to what each needed to quell the tension. They could have stated their anxiety was up when it was recognized and asked for time out—not participate in discussing anything further until they felt more in control of themselves. These may seem like foreign approaches to relationship conversation, but no matter how foreign it is, it will remain that way until it is implemented.

RMJ is a silent and deadly relationship assassin.

What do I want?

Be open to explore.

This is one of the most important questions that I can ever ask myself.

If I want happiness, fulfillment, and a joy filled future, it is up to me.

If I want peace, travel, calmness, love, or success, it is up to me.

> ## Asking *what I want* is a powerful question.

Otherwise, I go down life's highway with the world telling me where I am going and what I can have. Asking empowers me to be strategic and intentional about who I am, where I am going, and how I show up. It is a wonderful question to explore.

I oversee the rest of my life.

When I know where I am going and identify the tasks and behaviors I need to change to get there, it creates excitement. ***Change is difficult, but when I change with the intention of creating something new and better, it is amazing. I want to give my dreams a chance.***

Too many times, I want other people to change to facilitate my dreams or future. The only thing wrong with that is I cannot change them. When I have the erroneous idea that I can, I will frustrate them and myself.

I can influence others to change but I cannot change them. *They must answer for themselves, "What do I want?"*

Change is easy to resist. Wanting or desiring others to change is an effortless approach to change. Changing myself is difficult. This difficulty causes me to steer clear of powerful opportunities to grow and create a better future.

Changing the way I react or expect others to react can be liberating. By being forthright and genuine about how I want things to look, setting good goals, and adhering to them will give me a chance to change.

Weekly Display—knowing what you want...
Change my Actions and Behaviors to Change my Habits

To know what I need to change; I need to know what I want. Once I know what I want, the next step is to look at small actions and behaviors I can change to give it an opportunity. Changing a few small actions or behaviors daily can create successful new habits. Once I identify the actions and behaviors, I can monitor them on a consistent or regular basis to track progress. Then I can identify things that are working well and things that are not working well. When I can tell my story about being intentional and strategic in my efforts, I find myself motivated to do more.

Success breeds success.

Showing up differently, gives me the opportunity to have what I say I want.

I am stuck until I change myself. [BLIND SPOT]

I love the example set by a young man some time ago. He had a difficult circumstance in his family and felt like he was not included or important as others.

I will call him Jason. One afternoon Jason and I were talking. He was 12 when we began to discuss matters about feeling isolated and alone within his family. As I asked 'gently curious' questions pertaining to how he wanted his family to be different, he quickly replied, *"I want peace in my family."* I asked again and he said, *"I want to be praised."* When I ask him a third time, he said, *"I want a happy family."*

I was amazed by his desires. I wrote these things down quickly and was astonished. I then asked gently, *"What behaviors or actions can you change to give it a chance?"*

The key to success here was not looking for others to change but looking at what he could do differently to give what he wanted an opportunity to change. The actions/behaviors he came up with were remarkable. See figure WD1 on page 81 for the *Weekly Display* that we structured for him to see how his effort towards change could affect his circumstances.

When Jason began to modify and alter his behavior, everything changed slowly over time. He has given himself an opportunity to have what he says he wants...happiness, peace, and praise. **This effort manifests new habits.** As this change cultivates new habits over time, they can be dropped off the display.

At the end of the week, he summarized his achieved results and compared it to his goal. Then the following questions were answered...*what worked well this week, what didn't work well, and what do I want to focus on next week?*

The next chart is six weeks later. After a few weeks, the last items on his list were all hitting near 100% and were dropped off the chart. Extra reading, chores, and saying good things about his parents replaced the dropped items. This process continues until the habits have been changed and the "what do you wants" are obtained.

With this intentional strategic approach to change, he now has the prescription for major change that can positively impact him for a lifetime. It is even more powerful when you have a mentor or coach to hold you accountable.

What do you want?

What small changes in attitude, actions, or behaviors are you willing to begin to give it a chance?

The goals that you set for your daily focus could be everyday activities, hours, minutes, miles, pounds, pages read or any other things that you would like to measure.

The *Weekly Display* is the best key to focusing on change that I have found. See figure WD2 on page 82 for results.

Get your free downloadable weekly display at
www.jerrydclark.com/weeklydisplay

● Figure WD 1—**Weekly Display**[3]

Weekly Display that was structured to see how his effort towards change could affect his circumstances.

Change my Actions and Behaviors to Change my Habits
Date: 4 /27/21

What do I want?   I want a happy family/ I want to be praised/ I want peace in my family

My Daily Focus	Mon	Tue	Wed	Thu	Fri	Sat	Sun	Goal	Achieved	Net
no fits	0				0	0		5	4	-1
get along with sister	0	0	0	0	0		0	2	0	-2
don't do stupid things	0	0	0				0	4	2	-2
leave others alone when requested			0		0	0		7		-4
do nice things for my parents		0	0	0				5		0
say good things about myself								5	0	0
no detention					+0			0		
keep homework current								5		-1
be early for class								5		
make good grades								5		
be nice to friends								5		+2

What worked well this week? _mostly be nice to friends and school work_

What didn't work well? _things with my sister and doing school. it was confusing done alone_

What do I want to focus on next week? _doing things with my sister my parents and school coming_

● Figure WD 2—**Weekly Display Results**[3]

Weekly Display that was filled out to show his results towards change and how they affected his circumstances.

Change my Actions and Behaviors to Change my Habits
Date: 11/8/21

What do I want?   I want a happy family/ I want to be praised/ I want peace in my family

My Daily Focus	Mon	Tue	Wed	Thu	Fri	Sat	Sun	Goal	Achieved	Net
no fits	1		0	0	0	1	0	5	4	-1
get along with sister	0	0	0	0	0	1	0	2	1	-1
don't do stupid things	0	0	0	0	0	1	0	4	2	-2
leave others alone when requested	1	1	1	1		1	1	7	6	+1
do nice things for my parents			0		0			5	6	+1
say good things about myself	30	20	15	0	0	15	0	5	800	-10
Extra reading								90 min		-2
Do all chores	1	1	0	0	0	1	0	4		-2
Say good things about my parents								5	3	-2

What worked well this week? good day on Saturday. nealite do nice things for my parents

What didn't work well? things with my sister doing stupid things leave others alone

What do I want to focus on next week? leave others alone each day good things about my parents, boy good with parents

Build a better family

Intellectual and emotional maturation

It is 6:30 in the evening and dad is sitting in his brown leather easy chair watching the news and reading a magazine. He has had a stressful day at work and there are stressors at home. He is ready to decompress, relax, and see what he can do to feel human again.

His eight-year-old son is playing on the floor. He has been anticipating dad's return home. He loves his dad and feels safe and connected when he is engaged with him. He asked dad repeatedly to play a video game. Dad cunningly excuses his son's request and continues lost in his own world of recovery. The boy, knowing how this verbal game is played, continues relentlessly asking for dad to play.

Dad's annoyance was escalating. He is unconsciously venturing out of emotional control. He is becoming more and more annoyed. He is also oblivious to his part in this verbal game of avoiding communication or connection. [BLIND SPOT] He continues to reply that he will play in just a minute.

Finally, out of exasperation, as dad was looking at a large picture in a magazine, an idea struck him. He saw a picture of a family reunion consisting of about fifty people of assorted ages. He tore the entire page out, ripped it up in small pieces, handed the pieces to his son and told him as soon as he could get the picture, now a puzzle, back together that he would play a game with him.

In a matter of minutes his son came back and told the dad that he had completed the task. Much to his surprise the dad saw that the picture was completed. When dad asked his son how he did that so quickly, the boy told him that he had noticed on the backside of the family reunion picture, as his dad was tearing it, was a picture of a mom and dad. The boy continued, *"When I put the mom and dad together correctly, the whole family came together."* This is an old but significant story. When the mom and dad are emotionally healthy and operate as a cohesive unit, everything comes together. When they show honor, respect, dignity, love, care, intellect and emotional maturity, the whole family comes together. When decisions are made that have the best interest of the children in mind, the family strengthens.

How do you build a healthy family?

How do you create a family that has strength, confidence, courage, peace, love, and resilience?

How do you build a family that meets life head on with strategic and intentional purpose?

Before you can build a better family, one that is healthy and sound, the parents must be intellectually and emotionally mature. Like it or not, the parents are the leaders in the family. Demonstrate how you want your children to be. Act in a manner you want your children to emulate. Know when to bare down and when to relinquish. Show just enough emotion to get your point across. Be available and equipped. If you do not know an answer, show them how to find it. Separate any offense from the child. Love the child and dislike the bad deed.

Don't die on every hill, that is making everything a big battle.

There must be a clear line of communication and not competition between the parents. There must be understanding, support, common goals, and the ability to recognize their own strengths and weaknesses, melding them into a common future that unites and does not divide.

Remember the coal miners in Virginia who took canaries into the mines with them? They kept a close observation of how the canaries were acting. If they chirped and sang, the air was pure. When they stopped and sometimes died, it was a sign of toxic gas, and they needed to exit the mine immediately or die. I say we need a canary in our home to signify when the atmosphere is toxic and warn us of the potential dangers. *What or who can represent your canary in your home?*

> ## The best gift you will ever give your children is to love your spouse.

Family as Teams

Complex social systems

In looking at my family, what makes it great?

What is my participation in my family success?

What are my children saying about me, my spouse, my relationship?

Am I modeling the relationship I want for them?

> **Families are complex social systems consisting of individuals with their unique interpersonal struggles.**

Families are comprised of individuals who have different personalities and different ways of handling stress.

Parents have different emotional maturity levels and are at various intellectual platforms.

They come from different backgrounds, histories, and experiences.

Their exposure to life situations and trauma is different.

Their relationships with their parents may be different.

Exposure to drugs and alcohol may be different.

Their relationships with in-laws may be different.

As you can see, our past has an immense impact on everyone's overall health and emotional maturity level.

Education is another factor to be considered. We have a great education system. We have the ability to study almost anything to advance our careers and do well in the marketplace. Just name a career, and there is education designed for it. However, where do we study families, relationships, and parenting? These very important subjects seem to be omitted from our education system. For example, how do we educate ourselves for life questions like:

How do I know how to be a great husband?

How do I measure great parenting?

How do I evaluate if my family is socially and emotionally healthy?

How do I determine if I am growing my family to be who I want them to be?

How do I measure if I am strengthening my children to face life circumstances in a way that will not cause them pain or suffering?

How do I know I am giving them my best so they can have the best start in their lives?

What are my goals for myself as parent?

What are my goals for my children before they leave home?

Without knowing the answer to these questions, it will be difficult to build a healthy family. I get to be intentional and strategic about what I want to have happen. Building confident children will strengthen their possibilities for success.

Healthy families are a product of children learning how to become independent and parents learning how to let go. Neither job is easy. Independence is based on child development.

Children naturally learn to become independent as they learn to dress themselves, brush their own teeth, and tend to their executive functions that are important in childhood. These executive functions if not taught, will become stumbling blocks for the road ahead. As they grow into teenagers, their independence begins to change. This necessary change leads to conflict that can be healthy or unhealthy.

> **It is a delicate challenge to hold on and let go at the same time, like fishing, knowing when to pull and when to allow slack.**

A major difficulty for parents, occurs when a child or adolescent feels like he is in charge and knows more than the parents. This model is known as a *"parentified child."* This is a child who assumes the same power as the parent. They can argue and debate or fuss with equal authority. Their method is that of a very immature child who hooks the parents into an argumentative or combative role. [BLIND SPOT]

If we choose to follow his argument, we lower our thinking to a childlike or teenage behavior. Acting from this lowered level causes us to make decisions more out of childlike emotions rather than adult intellect.

Since their birth, I have had dreams for my children. I give up my dreams of what I want for them to allow them to have their own dreams as they become adults ***by learning to create an environment of letting go.***

Letting go for some parents is extremely difficult especially in today's world. Children and teens expect the freedom to go where they want to go, with whom they want to go with, and stay however long they want. Setting good limits where both parents are on the same page, leads to a healthy launching. If parents do not let go, and if adolescents do not become independent, then there is an occurrence where parents choose to take care of their adult children longer than they desire or should.

Letting go in a healthy manner, creates strong parents and strong young adults. Some adolescents and young adults are eager to be launched and gladly have their own lives. Some are naturally afraid. The more confident and the better they feel about themselves, the easier it is for them to launch. This is hard to think of when they are small children, and we are doing things that do not foster a confident young person or a strong sense of self. As children are being corrected and informed along their journey, it is important to remember how we want them to be when they are launched from the platform of their front door.

Example: Sometimes a very sobering conversation comes up when I hear conflict between parents and their adolescent children. I firmly believe parents do the best they know how to do with the idea of launching their children to be safe and productive citizens. Some parents are more equipped for this than others.

I love to paint a scenario of their son or daughter graduating high school. They are having an outdoor party with all their friends and family and the graduate's friends all present. It is a celebratory party with great food, laughter, and festivity.

At some point the graduate stands up and taps on his tea glass and invites everyone to sit down and says, *"Let me tell you about my dad or let me tell you about my mom."* At that point I ask the question,

"What would you like to hear them say?"

This question usually seems a surprise like they have not thought of this. [BLIND SPOT] In general, the answer includes things like: *"I want them to say they were loved. They were given the best support ever. They were encouraged. They were disciplined in a way that included teaching and molding. They feel equipped. They feel like we gave them our best."*

The follow up question to then ask is, **"Who writes the script the children used to talk about their parents?"** The answer to that question is the parents write the script. Interestingly enough, we all write the script other people use to talk about us. That's good news and bad news. The bad news is we may not have taken this into consideration up until now. The good news is if we know what we want them to say, then we can give them the experiences to give it a chance. There is no guarantee they will say what we want to hear.

Teenagers can be very young emotionally, and some act much more mature than their age. Age and emotional maturity for teenagers and young adults can vary drastically. Some 12-year olds can be more emotionally mature than an 18-year-old. I suggest steering them from their emotional maturity, not their physical age.

I also suggest having a minimum number of house rules. School should be their focus followed by maintaining the household. Then respect would follow these which would include respect for authority, others in the household, and themselves. [See Spirit of the Family, page 110]

The preparation for launching should begin very early, with the idea being, a release of confident, independent, and successful young adults.

Hierarchical Issues
The delicate balance in families.

In healthy families, parents are at the pinnacle of the household. Parents cannot be split in the decision-making process. Kids are allowed to go between the parents but never allowed to come in between them. It seems almost innate for a child to ask one parent for something and if they do not get what they want, go to the other parent. When parents are not in harmony, requests by the children can cause parental conflict, allowing the child to get their way while the parents debate, argue, or fight. In certain situations, (as I mentioned earlier) I see children have the same authority as the parents, the authority to tell the parents what needs to happen or not happen. Children want parents to be in charge, but parents must earn the right. If parents don't take the authority, the children will.

> **Knowing how the parents will make decisions,
> is important for the children.**

As children in the middle years grow older, they will ask for, and certainly should be allowed, more autonomy, and their opinions should be considered when decisions are made; however, parents are the final authority. Being clear and consistent with their boundaries is essential. Knowing how the parents will make decisions, is important for the children. It is healthy when children know what mom or dad will say or decide on a particular subject. A great question to ask when presented with something that is beyond the parents' limit would be, *"How do you think I will answer your question?"*

Parents often have a difficult time saying yes or no definitively. The ability to know what will produce vibrant, confident young adults is difficult when children are small. Being too lenient can create entitlement. Being too rigid can create rebelliousness. Be clear of the decision you have made, and do not become defensive or apologetic. You won't always be popular, but they are still going to love you. I like the rule being *'clear, consistent, and do not convince.'*

When I'm clear and consistent, children will know when they ask something of me what my general response will be. If I find myself in convinced mode, I find myself trying to prove to someone what they don't want to hear and what I do not want to give up. In turn they are trying to prove to me what they want and do not want to give up also.

> ## There is a delicate balance between setting limits and teaching how to negotiate.

Hierarchical issues also occur when a young couple marries and begins to have a family of their own. In healthy families, it is important for young parents, when beginning their own families, to learn to step up on an equal footing with their parents and function in an adult-to-adult relationship (just as neighbors function), otherwise they can be children raising children. It is important, after having your own children, to be the authority in your family. Grandparents, in healthy families, can offer but have no vote as how to raise your family. ***Otherwise, it's easy to find yourself in conflict, and sometimes it is a silent conflict which is the most dangerous.*** [BLIND SPOT]

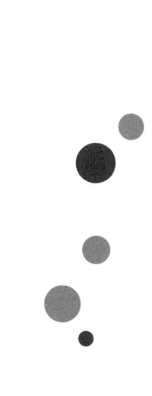

Families in Relationship

Building confidence

To build a better family, we must include the emotional effects that permeate all social systems.

When conflict, anxiety, or chaos happens, family relationships are heavily influenced. No matter the family dynamics, anxiety and intellect/spirituality compete for the same brain resources. Anxiety up, intellect/spirituality down. [See *Diagram 1*— page 28]

Individual emotional maturity requires one to be aware of his own emotions and regulate them effectively. They must also be aware of emotions of others and deal with them appropriately. Failure to do so may cause the feeling of being controlled by others or create an opportunity for conflict.

An emotionally mature family is not a collection of emotionally mature family members. Read that again, just because you have emotionally mature individuals does not ensure an emotionally mature family. *Family emotional maturity is not about suppressing negative emotions. It is about bringing emotions purposefully to the surface and understanding how they affect the family's health.*

Before family emotional maturity can come into play, the emotional maturity of the parents must be present. If not present, there cannot be an emotionally mature family. Family emotional maturity is about building relationships within the family and strengthening the family's ability to face challenges. Family emotional maturity means embracing and ultimately relying on the ever present and usually overlooked or mishandled emotions within the family.

**Individuation is a healthy concept
in emotional maturity.**

Individuation is a psychological separation of intellect, emotion, and independence of self from others. It means being able to be guided by your own thoughts or emotions and not by others emotions. The greater the persons level of individuation, the more they can act from their own core under any circumstance. The individuation process requires learning to think for oneself, independent of pressures, and loyalties of the family social system.

The opposite of individuation is fusion.

Being fused is the difficulty of separating self from others or being fused with family negative emotional patterns. Fusion cripples the ability to separate from others' moods, so it will not allow negative moods to permeate the family system. When a fused family member experiences negative emotions emitting from another, they join that mood.

Emotional maturity creates better decisions, more creative solutions, and higher morale, thus building a healthier family. It enhances families' participation, cooperation, and collaboration. Best of all, it builds trust.

Trust is the glue in relationships.

By employing the principles of family emotional maturity, they nurture and protect in a developmentally appropriate manner. It encourages each member to his or her highest potential as a person. Ideally, both the individual and the family are non-competitive, non-manipulative and free from hidden agendas. However, in real life, all families must manage some level of chronic anxiety and underlying family conflict. If this is unaddressed, it worsens and weakens the family.

47 on the Algebra test

I was privileged to work in a hospital setting getting the experience of all kinds of psychological matters. I facilitated multifamily groups of adolescents, children, and their parents. These children and adolescents were there for issues of behavior, drugs, alcohol, depression, anxiety, or other circumstances that cause life and families to be out of balance. Many wonderful things happen in multifamily groups that do not happen in regular family groups. In multifamily groups the observers in the family can see the things that cause other people's problems. They can see things that other people are doing that they cannot see in themselves or in their own families. This observation allows them to identify their own blind spots.

One Saturday morning, there were about 6 adolescents and their families present. Family members were updated by their adolescents during that time. After the group started, one dad who came in late, interrupted the group by asking his son what he made on his algebra test. The boy replied 47. Immediately, the dad almost left his chair and began to berate the boy about not studying, not being engaged, failing in life, not having his priorities straight, and on and on and on. [BLIND SPOT]

I noticed the boy wanted to say something but did not. I asked the young man what he had to say. At first, he didn't want to divulge anything, but then said, *"I just wanted to tell my dad that 47 was the highest grade in the class."* A hush fell on the group. The dad set back with his chin in his chest and didn't say another word.

Sometimes it is easy to overreact or fly off the handle.

Sometimes we don't listen well.

Sometimes our intention of being a great parent gets overridden by our emotions.

This dad is not a bad dad. He wanted his son to excel. He didn't realize how he was an impediment to his son's success. This kind of sustained parental behavior is a good example of how a child or an adolescent's spirit gets broken. Here is an opportunity to feel worthless and sometimes go through life with that miserable feeling of I do not matter, I'm not enough, I could never please dad, boss, spouse, or myself. All of this creates terrible anguish fueled by anxiety overriding intellect/spirituality.

Families are very complex systems, requiring especially the parents, to be in control of themselves. Self-control for all family members is essential for healthy, emotional families.

Cut from the herd

Can't live with them. Can't live without them.

This is my "West Texas" term, referring to isolation, dismissal, or rejection. "Cut from the herd" is when one member of the family is excluded from the rest. In nature, animals establish herds for protection against their predators and are safe because the herd protects each other. Being outside the herd yields no protection and animals are subject to the hazards of life.

Sometimes the herd cuts us out.
Sometimes we cut ourselves out.

Regardless of how we find ourselves outside the herd, it is extremely dangerous.

Families are weakened when they are fractured. It's easy to withdraw when words, actions, or harsh experiences exist, giving the experience of not being enough.

Sometimes, it is necessary to cut someone from the herd because of their poor choices, such as drugs, alcohol, sexual, verbal, or physical abuse. Cutting someone from the herd for these reasons protects those within the herd, helps teach the person who has been cut that this behavior weakens and threatens the health of the herd and will not be tolerated. Setting limits and expecting great things from all family members is extremely important.

If you find yourself cut from the herd, it is essential that you look for the blind spots that are invisible to you in the moment.

Strong herds are powerful
and regenerate strength.
Families are the same.

Triangulation and Coalitions

Put an end to the drama.

As mentioned in *Hierarchical Issues, pg. 95,* parents in healthy families are at the pinnacle of the household and are not to be split by the children. When anxiety occurs between two or more family members, it creates fractures and distance. This generates opportunities for *triangulation or coalitions,* and if left to their own devices become blind spots, causing even more anxiety. Let us take a look at these potential blind spots.

Triangulation

This occurs when there is conflict or misunderstanding between two people. Rather than deal one-to-one with the responsible person, a third person is pulled into the conversation and the results become unhealthy for all three. In healthy family relationships, a one-to-one relationship exist with each member of the family, rather than having relationships with someone in the middle.

Example: Mom and dad have been married for 15 years and their son Joey is twelve. He is doing relatively well in school, but there is difficulty at home. Dad seems to be more the authoritarian than mom.

The more he gets harsh and tough with Joey, the more lenient mom becomes. Joey and dad do not get along and mom continues to intervene. In discussions, she generally takes Joey's side. The difficulty began when the parents argued rather than worked through this issue. Arguments, in this case, solve nothing and only polarize the parents. Joey feels caught in the middle and becomes anxious. If this pattern continues, over time it can produce permanent anxiety. It also causes parents to have continuous frustration that intensifies their resentments. [See Rust in Relationships, page 140]

Coalitions

Blended families are a family unit where one or both parents have children from a previous relationship, but they have combined to form a new family. ***Nuclear families*** are a family group consisting of parents and their children (one or more).

Coalitions appear in many ways. In unhealthy families, coalitions might exist between one parent and children against the other parent. It could be one parent and child or children against another parent, child, or children.

In blended families, many times, it is the two nuclear families against the other. In these coalitions, the good is not the focus, and it is the bad brought out, thus inciting family deterioration.

Coalitions create separation, build walls, produce double standards, and breed opportunities for arguments and division. Coalitions are easy to spot because it is one faction against the family or one faction against another person.

In a healthy family, the strong coalition is between mom and dad. Children, no matter what the age, do not come between them. Mom and dad are not always going to agree but, for family health, mom and dad must stand beside each other and support one another in the face of family conflict.

Private conversation behind closed doors may be necessary after such interaction.

Example: In some situations, I see one parent being too harsh or too lenient, and the other parent intervening during that process. This causes extreme confusion for the children and lets them know that the family hierarchy is fractured. Generally, an argument will ensue between the parents and the kids can go away getting by with what was going on to begin with.

In this circumstance, I invite the parent who is hearing the excessive harshness or leniency going on between the other parent and the child or children to present themselves standing next to the other parent. This parent comes into the room, stands by the other parent as though they have no agenda whatsoever. They do not look at their opposite parent. They do not look at the children. They do not do anything to cause attention to themselves, but only stand there in the most innocuous way. This creates a situation where the parent giving directions to the children becomes more self-contemplative. The children are seeing a situation where both parents are standing side by side and presenting an intimidating duo. It is not unusual for the parent being too harsh or lenient to begin to see how they are showing up and may even relent.

After the parent, who was originally tending to the children, finishes with their business, the children are dismissed with their instructions. The parents can then retire to the bedroom and discuss what just happened.

They may not agree, but it is a great opportunity to use this situation as an example of how both parents might see the situation from their own perspectives. This is a good time for both to share their views, not convince, but have a private discussion about what has just happened and what would be best for the children.

This is not an easy task, and it requires practice. In fact, it is extremely difficult. It is easy to want to make it about an argument and want to prove the other parent wrong. It is easy to become polarized and be right and attempt to convince the other parent he/she is wrong. This is neither the time nor place to go there. It requires compromise and forgiveness. It requires the two people to be extremely interested in what is best for the children.

Strong parental coalitions build extraordinarily healthy and secure families.

Spirit of the Family

An identified rally point.

At times, families are blindly fractured by sarcasm, put downs, blame, shame, yelling or other negative actions. Other times, I notice families are fractured by their many differing points of view. Some individuals are more focused on themselves than the family. Unity and cohesion are missing. Establishing the spirit of the family is an approach that provides focus, a common direction, and builds a healthy family.

I like the idea of utilizing the "spirit of the family" to help look at the overall picture of what is taking place in the family. *How do parents want the family to function or what is the spirit of this family?*

The "spirit of the family" might be words like respect, peace, harmony, joy, love, care, or any word that the family could rally around to encourage and create solidarity. If it is not specifically expressed, it can manifest into something very negative.

> ## The "spirit of the family" is usually undeclared but present.

Cutting comments, put downs, blame, sarcasm, and fear can permeate a family and be interpreted to be the undeclared spirit of the family. When the constructive idea of the "spirit of the family" comes along, there is a choice in the way the family interacts, communicates, perceives, and feels toward one another. It can eliminate agony, blame, pain, misunderstanding, anxiety, and frustration.

Focusing on the spirit of the family can create hope which is so commonly missing in families. Knowing that with every breath, and every word spoken, we are intentionally choosing the potential outcome of family members to feel safe, secure, and healthy. The words to implement this spirit can be soft and gentle or very challenging depending on the circumstances.

Do our words lift or tear down the family or its members?

When we choose to operate outside the spirit of the family, the family becomes unhealthy. The spirit of the family directs all conversations, communications, and actions without numerous rules. This allows each family member to see if he/she is operating within the spirit of their household. Each member can easily identify when they are in violation of the spirit, as well as others recognizing who is within or without the spirit.

The benefit of having a "spirit of the family" is everyone knows what is expected and everyone can line up behind it. If they choose not to operate within the spirit, they could be cut from the herd or take some time alone to figure out ways of reconnecting with others within the spirit of the household.

The interesting thing about declaring a spirit of the family is that it continuously focuses on how each should act. It gives an opportunity for each one to compare their actions and behaviors to the spirit of the family.

It allows the home to be the sanctuary.

Our home is a place of peace, kindness, instruction, learning, joy, love, and care, not hostility, anger, or sarcasm. It is not a place where individual spirits are broken, and confidence is minimized, but a place where all are uplifted. ***Family members become intentional about catching others doing things right and well.***

This creates another dynamic that will need to be addressed. There must be a time to air grievances, settle disputes and hurt feelings with a more productive approach. Parents, need to correct violations of the spirit of the household. Corrections are essential and healthy. The spirit of the family is a balance, catching people doing things right as well as catching them doing things wrong.

This value-added concept, adopting the idea of the *"spirit of the family,"* is like any major change and can be difficult but not impossible to implement. It is like the flywheel affect, or the lift off stage of a Saturn rocket, taking a lot of effort to propel the spirit of the household into a new orbit.

Resistance is to be expected; it will be necessary to stay clear and consistent on the spirit of the household. It is the spirit of the household that can ensure each individual is held in high esteem and differences are appreciated.

The spirit of the family allows parents to maintain control and build a better family team. The spirit of the household allows parents to maintain a sense of control through healthy authority.

What is the source f the problem?

Anxiety up, Intellect Down

Something interesting happened when a family lodged several complaints against their son. He was not keeping his room clean, not taking good care of his homework, not doing any chores around the house, getting in trouble at school, arguing, and many other rebellious deeds. The dialogue between the parents consisted of finding proof of all the bad things that this young man was doing. The son is 10 years old.

I asked them to begin by looking at things he is doing right and well. It is so easy to focus on the negative attitude and behavior.

We can influence change, but we cannot change them.

Looking at our own behavior and showing by example what we expect, we can begin to see change and modify their behavior.

This young man was being disrespectful by talking back, running from her and being defiant to her request. I asked the mom if she would record the interaction she had when the son was demonstrating this kind of behavior.

She said she had just bought a new camcorder (this was many years ago) and would be glad to get proof. The next session, she and her son attended, Mom pulled out her camcorder, and with a big smile said, *"I got him!"*

The three of us began to look at the tiny little screen on the camcorder to see him acting out, talking back, and escaping under the bed. The next thing we saw was the mom going out of control, yelling, and screaming at him. In an out-of-control approach, she was telling him what an awful young man he was, threatening him with loss of fun things, and even grounding him. Suddenly, she began to see the ineffectiveness of her efforts and how highly unsuccessful they were. After about a minute of watching this, the mom said, *"Can we please turn this off."* She had seen who she was in this situation, and it was a tremendous revelation.

She was able to see from the recording what she could not see in the moment of crisis. We do not see our actions nor hear our voice in our conversations or our arguments. Our attempt to convince someone of something is out of our comprehension until we see the recording. Anxiety up, intellect/spirituality down.

What would it be like to witness ourselves in an argument?

What would it be like to record your conversation whenever there is conflict, and then listen to it by yourself?

It gives you a chance to hear the voice you have not heard yet. You hear the other voice but not your own. It can be a colossally revealing event to hear yourself in a heated conversation. Some may ask, *"Do you think I would act this way if I knew it was being recorded?"* Probably not. But take notice, if we know it is being recorded, we want to perform well and produce something that sounds eloquent and intelligent, as opposed to unintelligent, anxious, or even angry.

There is an old song we could sing here,
"Oh yes, I'm the great pretender..."[4]
pretending we are our best selves in any
circumstance or situation.

The sole purpose of the recording is to hear your own voice, not use the recording against another. Recordings can be extremely beneficial if they are done with the idea of everyone getting to listen to it by themselves, and then they can be erased. Blind spots can be uncovered with this form of viewing ourselves with the idea of building a better me.

Points of View
Different Perspectives
The truth we know...

Looking at conflicts from multiple points of view and perspectives can be enlightening. At times, our mind gets in the way when we are looking at or accepting new possibilities. Often, we desire to hang on to the truth we know, seeking to prove the other wrong, as opposed to graciously considering their differing perspective or point of view. I can respect your point of view and keep mine also.

Look at the illusion of the old woman and the young woman.

Anonymous illustrator in late 19th century Germany. William Ely Hill (1887 - 1962), a British cartoonist.

The picture does not change. There are two distinct women depicted here. This is an amazing example of not right or wrong but having a different perspective.

Too many times we argue about superfluous issues.

Real problems get buried in the self-conversation of *"I'm not going to say anything because I do not want to cause more trouble."* This avoidance then builds the bomb that will eventually go off at an inopportune time.

Attempting to make sense of someone else's point of view can link to high anxiety, especially if I believe I am right, and you are without a doubt wrong. Think back to the discussion on anxiety being on a continuum from mild, to severe, to chronic. Operating out of mild anxiety, my voice may raise a little, or I may push my point of view a little. If I am in a severe or chronically anxious state, I may get into threatening or belligerent mode, which may lead to severe harm or even worse. [BLIND SPOT]

On this continuum, my decision can create calm or chaos. My choices will be healthy or unhealthy. It will lead to intellect/spirituality up, anxiety down or to anxiety up, intellect/spirituality down. The same with reptilian brain, we noticed when animals or reptiles began to get stressed or threatened, they posture themselves physically and vocally in a manner to subdue the threat or opposition.

Our reptilian brain is for survival only, not for relationship building.

Remember our discussion about the animal kingdom: a lion or an elephant would posture themselves to look bigger to gain superiority and overpower their opposition. Operating out of this part of the brain can only lead to poor relationships.

In talking of relationships, I mean familial relationships not relationships that occur in war, rugby, or any game of extreme competition. When conflict arises because of points of view and differing perspectives being challenged, we need to enforce self-control. We are all unique individuals with distinctive backgrounds and life experiences. Our perspectives need to be respected and valued not condemned or cheapened.

> **You always have a choice; make the choice to bridge the divide.**

'Why' in relationships, can be the first step to a fight.

Prove it to me, I bet you can't!

The *'why'* question is charged with frustration, emotion, hidden agendas, and sometimes anger.

'Why' is not a gently curious question. The why question can be the beginning of the downfall of communications in a relationship. I never ask *'why'* in relationships.

'Why' in relationship is caustic.

I say it means, prove to me and I bet you can't. The why questions are examples of how our culture allows us to maintain a sense of anxiety, defensiveness, or frustration. Rather than asking the *'why'* question, I suggest making a statement about yourself. If there is tension because someone didn't call, it is easy to ask, *"Why did you not call?"* I contend there is no answer to this that will satisfy the anxiety or frustration of the one asking. It is cultural to look at the other person rather than to look inside. *'Why'* provokes and puts people on the defensive. *'Why'* is asking for justification that usually cannot remedy anxiety.

"Why did my car not start?" is a good *'why'* question. *"Why is this apparatus not working?"* is a good question, and there are good answers for both of those questions.

The *'why'* in relationships can stir or aggravate emotions without any knowledge or care for how we come across to the other person.

A novel approach would include identifying an internal reason for asking. Rather than ask *"Why did you not call?"* I could talk about myself and provide rich information to connect and not repel. I feel the genuine conversation within myself has to do with...I was worried, I wanted to hear your voice, I missed you, I was afraid something could have happened to you. All these comments would be legitimate and more engaging rather than the *'why'* question.

Let's explore the *'why'* question in relationships.

Why did you not call?

Why are you late?

Why are you driving so fast or slowly?

Why are you looking at me that way?

These and other similar *'why'* questions are the preludes to an uncomfortable or maybe even difficult argument or disagreement.

Examination of this generally shows that the person who asked the question has anxious energy on the circumstance or situation. The question *"Why are you late?"* is an expression to say that I'm frustrated with you, unhappy, feel unimportant, or I feel like you have caused me inconvenience. I don't really care why, as much as I want the circumstance not to reoccur and to let you know I am upset.

In looking at the question, it is obvious that the person asking the question was operating from some sort of negative emotion being that of frustration, worry, concern, abandonment, cut from the herd, or unappreciated. Rather than talk about that themselves, they ask the why question of which there's no good answer.

A further dissection of what's going on behind the scenes could be the one asking the question (feeling like an attacker) was concerned, wanted to hear your voice, know that you were safe, to be acknowledged by connection. Rather than make these kinds of statements, which would cause joining or connection, we culturally asked the question *'why'?* *"Why were you late?"* could be translated as a statement rather than a question, by saying *"I was looking forward to seeing you, hearing your voice, seeing your smile, feeling your touch"* which is noticeably more forthright and engaging, than *"Why were you late?"*

Instead of *'why'* ask gently curious questions:

"Help me understand?"

"What else can you tell me about this?"

"I am confused; can you elaborate?"

They are the connecting questions—showing you care and empathize as opposed to condemning, blaming, or putting another person on the defense.

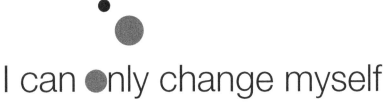

I can only change myself

Changed is inevitable, growth is optional. ~ *John C. Maxwell* [5]

His thoughts

I'm coming home from work and pulling in the driveway.

What will the atmosphere in the house be today?

I expect when I walk in, I will get a cursory hello and she will either be busy doing something around the house or looking at social media or participating in some other electronic distractions. The kids will say hi if they're not in their rooms occupying their own time with electronic devices or playing online with friends. I feel very under-appreciated and like all my efforts go unrecognized.

This is not the way it used to be.

Our household used to be happy and exciting.

It used to be fun. I once was greeted and hugged, but now it's different.

They just don't act like they used to act.

I work hard. I try to show my love. I think I am a good provider. I still try to give them everything and this is how I get treated?

Social media and other distractions have taken me out of the equation.

Her thoughts

Oh, I think he's driving up now; what will his mood be?

I wonder what he will see what I haven't done or should be doing.

I had better get up and act as though I'm doing something, or I will be judged and possibly accused of sitting here all day not doing anything.

He used to come home happy with a smile and give me a loving hug.

He will probably complain about what the children are doing or not doing.

I'm sure it will be my fault. Our household is so sad, so fractured and disconnected. I just feel lonely and disengaged. I miss so many great things we once enjoyed. I wish it could be like it used to be.

How does this story end? Unless change happens, this couple will continue to blame and accuse the other until one or both decide to end it.

Maybe this sounds familiar. I hope not, but if it does, I have found hope. It is so easy to see what the other person is doing or not doing that is causing problems in the relationship. It's easy to blame. It is easy to compare what they once did to what they do or not do today.

I must recognize that life is constantly changing.

After being in relationship for a while, it's easy to become comfortable and allow my bad habits to show up. When children come along, life changes drastically. The time we had as a couple has been drastically reduced. The demands of children are frequent and many. They require inordinate time and attention. Having to live in the moment with the demands of young children and even older ones, leaves little time for us as a couple to renourish and replenish our relationship. Working with the children and their schedules, schools, friends, and extracurricular activities are more demanding than I recognized. These things occur gradually overtime and it's easy to get over involved and over committed without even knowing it. At times, schedules call for the parents to have to be at different locations with different children.

Is there a way out of this dilemma? What is the answer?

I saw the major issue as wanting the other person to change. After all, change is horribly difficult and when I see that the other person can change and cause our life to be more pleasant, balanced, and joyful, it makes sense to make that request. Interestingly enough, they do not want to change for the same reasons. *I have discovered the secret to this dilemma is to change myself.*

Many times, in my office I am asked a question, *"Why am I the only one who has to change?"* or *"Why don't you pick on him/her?"*

It is so common for us to want the other person to change because it's so obvious the problem is not mine. Changing me is most difficult. It seems easier and more reasonable for the other to change.

Blind spots are those hidden actions or behaviors we are experiencing that do not work in our favor. Some examples are common things like, having to be in control or to be right, needing to correct the other person.

Blind spots cause enormous difficulties because we are unaware of their influence on our behavior. In a recent conversation with a young couple, the husband corrected his wife every comment she made. He would tell her that she was not right, she left out something, she needed to be sure all the facts were accurate. This was absolutely suffocating for her to hear. She shut down and gave him the impression that she approved. I frequently interrupted their conversation which was difficult. Both felt so right and were acting out of habit they had employed for the past 10 years.

As I identified his actions which were correcting her, he wanted to argue with me. When he would say "No" to something that she said and began to explain his version, I did my best to tell him that she was hearing that she was dead wrong. He began telling me "No," that I was wrong. As we continued the discussion, it was almost impossible for him to see that his logic, intellect and reasonability were excellent, yet the way he came across was totally repelling to her. It is difficult for people, in this situation, to see that they are repulsive because they feel so righteous, yet in this moment being right is pushing her away.

This kind of *'right'* I call *'Dead Right'*.

Perhaps out of frustration or retreating, she is now allowing poor behavior and causing him to continue to treat her in a way that is not healthy. Neither one is aware of the negative consequences they are contributing to the relationship. He still wanted to prove his point, which had merit, yet from the standpoint of fostering relationships was a killer. His ability to reason and use logic, which I call rationalize, minimize, and justify, was so damaging that neither of them knew how to recover. She had endured this for so long and was so frustrated that she was ready to end the relationship.

Not looking at this situation from fault or blame but looking at it from both person's standpoint, both played a major role in how the relationship was degrading. His inability to see what he was doing to repel her and her inability to see what she was doing to get her point across, caused both to be so frustrated that during this conversation the anxiety escalated to a point were both closed off to hearing any further feedback. Nothing was resolved.

I never got heartburn by swallowing my pride.

Here are two well educated people who could solve most any problem, yet from an emotional standpoint they could solve nothing. It gets back to the point of going out of control to gain control or not recognizing that the anxiety portion of the brain has taken over the intellect/spiritual portion mentioned earlier. This revelation to both was strange and difficult to ingest or to make sense of, because it was so foreign to their thinking.

We continued to discuss the damaging parts of their conversation as they occurred. It was difficult to stay in the conversation with them, allowing them to talk, as I continued to interject and input things that would help both to understand their contribution to the conflict.

I could see from his standpoint he was feeling that the story she was telling herself was making him look like a bad guy. This was difficult for him because he desired to look stellar for her. Her idea was not to condemn him, but to point out things that were not working for her. In her quest to get her point across, it only appeared to him that she was arguing and causing him to go into convince mode. Neither could see how convincing the other was working against them.

Convincing only clutters understanding.

Both began to shift from emotion to intellect and look within rather than at the other. The session ended with both reflecting this circumstance in a very different way. Both were open to looking for what they were doing that contributed to causing additional conflict and frustration as opposed to blaming and accusing the other. This gave an opportunity for creating more understanding in the conversation so that both could grow from this circumstance.

We are all blindsided by our innate bad habits in communications. It is difficult to change our thinking, our presentation and our understanding of how to have great conversations.

Ideas for changing who I am in conversation

Employ statements, such as, *"Let me tell you what I need from you before I tell you what I'm going to tell you."* When someone begins to talk and does not declare what they need from the listener, it can create chaos and disconnection. If the speaker's desire is to vent, and get things off his mind, and the listener thinks they need to be fixed, or receive suggestions to take care of their situation, anxiety will arise and if not dealt with appropriately will cause the conversation to decay.

Telling what they need will give both directions for a healthy conversation. It allows for intent to be declared and understanding to exist before the dialogue begins.

If the listener asks, *"What do you need from me?"* during the conversation before it goes too far, it also can result in understanding and connection rather than deterioration.

Ask yourself before speaking, *"How come I'm about to make this statement or ask this question?"* This is also a great way of looking at communication from the standpoint of the following:

"What is my motive?"

"What is my mission?"

"How come I am about to ask or present this?"

I can now guide the outcome that I'm looking for. The key is a desire to connect, showing vulnerability by divulging what is going on with me.

At the end of the day, all I can do is change my reaction, response, and behavior. No one else can do that for me or make me do it. I am learning to let things go and walk away from things that are hurting me. I am learning to pick my battles while being mindful of the bigger picture at hand. I am learning to bend rather than break. I may not be able to change other people or situations, but I can choose to increase my awareness and consistently work towards the person that I am finally becoming.

Remember, blind spots are gold mines.

When we explore, dig in, sift through, and discover our blind spots, our relational problems will dissipate. By overcoming our blind spots, we can create a closeness we did not know how to get to before.

Giving too much

We teach people how to treat us.

I get a chance to meet some of the nicest people in the world. People who are givers and do not have a clue how much they give.

Givers find takers and don't realize it.

Giving too much sounds like it should be rewarded, but it seems to have the opposite effect.

A woman meets a gentleman and would like to get a little more acquainted with him. She decides to invite him over for a meal and a movie. After a fine meal and great conversation, she jumps up and says let me put these dishes away and we'll go watch the movie. Generally, the other would ask, *"Can I help?"* which is answered quickly with, *"No I got this, I know where everything goes"* and within a short period of time the dishes are put away, table is cleaned off, and they retire to watch the movie.

Later she decides she would like to do that again; it was fun and invites him over again. After another fine dinner and great conversation, she jumps up and says, *"Let me put these dishes away and we'll go watch the movie."* He asks, *"Can I help?"* which she replies. *"Nope I got this. It will not take me but a minute to put this away and then we can watch the movie."* Both had another great evening, and this continues over time.

This time he comes over to her house. A great meal is cooked. They enjoy dining, laughing, and carrying on, and she says, *"Let me put*

these dishes away and we'll go watch the movie." He says, *"OK. I'll go start the movie."* She is now in her kitchen alone slogging through the dishes, wondering why she is doing this alone, and he is in the other room NOT HELPING! This does not seem right. [BLIND SPOT]
This is an example of how we teach people to treat us. Anytime someone asks us if they can help, the answer should be of course.

Generally, givers are people who enjoy being asked if they can help and get satisfaction by giving to another person and helping them in a situation. When you decide not to ask for help, you have robbed that person of the opportunity to feel good about their giving and sharing. It is difficult to see this in day-to-day life and in minute-to-minute conversation.

Some feel they have no voice in their relationships. When asking for help, the other person has an excuse or is reluctant. I may ask again, but with the same disparaging method of asking, without capitulation, I give up again.

In this situation, as in all communications, the sender of the message is responsible to determine if the message has been received. If not, it is the sender's responsibility to resend the message in a different and more understandable manner. If the message still has not been received, it's not the receiver's fault. The sender of the message is responsible to restructure the message in such a way they know the message was heard.

If it was conveyed, so that the other person understood what was being said or asked, then assess the request, the denial, or the dismissal. It is important to address this disrespect at the time and not allow it to be a resentment.

If I relent, I will resent.

When I resent, I pull away and do it myself, thus teaching the other person it is okay to deny my request. *When I treat myself with dignity and respect, I will not allow anyone to treat me differently.* Many times, I hear the statement, *"I've told them 10 times to do this, and they still don't do it until I scream or yell."* This tells me and them that the 1st 9 times it was okay to be ignored. I need to learn how to say it once with authority.

If I ask the children to pick up their shoes one time and they tell me they are going to do it, but do not, as soon as I get an opportunity, I will take possession of the shoes I asked to be picked up. I may put them in a place like the garage, the pantry, or my bedroom and when the person who needs the shoes is looking for them, I play detective. I ask, *"Where would they be if you had done what I asked?"* I might say, *"I picked them up and I put them somewhere. Perhaps if you look around a little bit you might find them."* This transfers the heat from me being upset with them. They did not mind my request, so I transfer the heat to them rather than trying to get my point across multiple times. A delayed consequence is counterintuitive and takes sustained practice.

Remember, we teach people how to treat us; make sure your message is heard. *By the way, saying the same thing louder is not an example of restructuring what I am trying to communicate.*

'Have to' versus 'Get to'

Major paradigm shift!

Many years ago, a good friend of mine, JD, from our church was having kidney failure and had to go to dialysis three times a week. His wife would get up early in the morning and take him at 3:30am. There were several of us from the church who would pick him up about 7:00 or 7:30. He would want to go to breakfast before taking him home.

JD was a rough old man. He was usually in a grumpy mood after dialysis. He complained when I picked him up in my truck because the step was too high, so I built a stool for him. This appeased him to some degree. Usually when I would take him to breakfast, he would complain about where we went, how bad the breakfast was, or how it could have been better.

This would occur week after week as I picked him up usually on Wednesdays. He was always in such a grumpy mood, and rightfully so, and if I was ever late, I was in trouble which I totally understood. All I heard was how hard it is to wait and how he didn't know if I was going to be there.

I was usually there early sitting in the waiting room with dialysis patients. I began to meet many of them because they came at the same time on Wednesdays. I started to hear their stories. "I can't empty my dishwasher anymore, or I can't reach the cabinets to put my dishes away, I can't vacuum anymore, I can't sweep, I hate it when the wind blows and my trash cans go down the street, I usually have to get someone to go get them for me."

This was the beginning of a major shift for me. I did not like to put the dishes away. I didn't like to empty the dishwasher, vacuum, sweep, nor chase the trash cans. As I sat there and listened to the stories, I began to look at my hands and feet. I began to think how equipped I am; what a privilege it is to have health, strength, and ability. At that moment I shifted 'I have to' to 'I get to.'

I 'have to' is a drudgery. I 'get to' is a privilege. I get to empty the dishwasher, sweep and chase the trash cans because I am equipped with a healthy body. I have two good hands and feet. If I think of it as a gift that I get to do something, life becomes easier. It is my choice to be involved and engaged in life.

Today, regardless of how much I do not want to do a chore, I remember that 'I get to.' ***What a privilege!***

Rust in Relationships

Listening beneath the words.

I call resentments *'rust'* in relationships.

This is a term I have coined to compare relationships that are in trouble, to a fine piece of metal that is rusting. *Rust is silent and destructive. Resentments are the same.* A fine car that is not maintained can rust and deteriorate in front of us, losing its value quickly. If left unmaintained, it will ruin. The longer the rust exists without attention, the more damage it causes. The longer resentments are not dealt with, the more corrosive the relationship becomes.

Example: The husband sees little things that are not going well. He thinks he has communicated to his wife what he needs from her. When change does not occur, he turns his attention away from her, thinking he has done what was needed even if no change occurred. If he says something that does not get tended to, he can then hold that against her and feel righteous. The problem does not go away.

Problematic or rusty relationships exist for many reasons. He drifted away by focusing on the children or his career. He stopped doing important things his wife desired. His voice became silent especially when his wife got loud. He blames her and waits for change that probably will not come. This results in poor maintenance and neglect which leads to a caustic relationship.

Resentments in relationships create avoidance, distance, and misunderstandings. It covers, insulates, and fractures the infrastructure of the relationship. They are silent, subtle, and often overlooked. Resentments are produced by what is said and what is not said. It can be what is assumed to be true rather than using a curious approach

142 Blind Spots...In Relationships

to seek understanding. I say, *"We are not so good at guessing each other's intentions."* Are we just having conversation or sharing words rather than looking for understanding, connection or improvements?

I observe that sometimes couples attempt to avoid conflict by not saying what they really think or feel. This is a myth. ***Silence or withholding information does not eliminate conflict. My experience is that it defers the conflict and builds a bigger bomb.*** When conflict arises, the bomb is an accumulation of all the things that were left unsaid, and it creates much more damage.

Relationships where couples avoid each other are subject to rust. Avoidance occurs by not talking, watching TV, talking on the phone, industriously focusing on the computer, reading, working late, doing volunteer work and many other ways.

Poor communications in a culture of educated people, seems to me to be the largest contributor in creating this kind of rust. If poor communication creates a problematic or rusty relationship, then it stands to reason healthy relationships are a result of honest open feedback. ***Perhaps honesty with compassion rather than brutally honest.***

If the woman in the relationship says, *"You don't ever listen to me,"* it is a natural reaction to argue, justify a position or give examples where listening did not take place. When the man takes this position, he silently, without saying it, tells her, *"You are wrong."* It is difficult to accept, so she goes silent or argues to convince him that he is wrong. Neither one wants to admit being wrong, so the argument ends with silence or another explosion, creating distance not closeness.

Resentment begins and rust takes a foothold.

Gently curious is a phrase used to gently identify true meaning and provide understanding. Too many times caustic questions or statements are allowed to steer the mood of the conversation. As a result, it is easy to attempt to justify or convince the other that a softer approach is needed. The intention or position could have been stated without being drawn into an uncomfortable conversation.

To do this, I employ a technique I call *'listening beneath the words.'* I should look for the meaning of the statement, *"You don't ever listen to me."* It can be translated *"You are very important to me, and I miss the conversation we once had."* It can mean, *"I miss you and I am feeling lonely."*

**Listening beneath the words
allows the listener to hear compliments
rather than complaints.**

If you want to polish your relationship, we learned earlier to ask 'gently curious' questions.

"Help me understand what you mean?"

"What else can you tell me about this?"

"Can you give me examples?"

Remember: *'why'* is not gentle, but hostile and accusatory.

As you ask these gently curious questions, then LISTEN for under-standing. Keep away from convincing mode to prove they are wrong. After gathering the data, ask them what they need from you.

This is a good time to say you want to process what was said, and you will get back with them. Leave with love. Upon your return, be careful because it is a great time for closeness and understanding. If closeness is unfamiliar, it could be easily sabotaged.

Look at a possible outcome if the *"You don't ever listen to me"* state-ment was handled in this manner:

Sarah says, *"You don't ever listen to me."*

John replies, *"Sounds like you are upset. What else can you tell me about this?"*

Sarah says, *"You just don't ever have time to talk anymore. Other things seem more important."*

John replies, *"Help me understand what you need from me."*

Sarah says, *"I just need to know I'm important to you and what I have to say matters. I need to feel pursued by you."*

John replies, *"I want you to know that I love you more than ever. Perhaps I haven't been letting you know this. Let me finish what I'm doing here, then I will show you how important you are to me."*

This is a difficult shift to make. It is a new way to process what is said or asked. The result produces much better understanding and the opportunity to connect, rather than creating more resentment and corrosion.

> **Oil that prevents rust in relationships consists of honesty, openness, and emotionally mature conflict resolution.**

Honesty needs to be compassionate rather than brutal. *Openness indicates all things said are true and nothing is withheld. Resolution to conflict is looking for agreement and compromise.*

A fine automobile comes with instructions for maintenance. Without scheduled maintenance, the warranty is voided. ***Do we place a higher priority on our mechanical things rather than our relationship? Heaven forbid!***

Cesspool versus heart...

Which do I fill?

After relationships have established themselves over the years, they sometimes become stale and fade. It is easy at that point to focus on the negative things that are going on in the relationship and overlook the positive.

When we establish a precedent of catching each other doing things wrong, it seems to be overwhelming and sometimes difficult to stop. The struggle with this is that by focusing on the negative, we tear each other down and set ourselves up to be torn down in return.

Early in relationships that is not the case. Early in the relationship we catch each other doing things right and well and use very little language pertaining to anything negative. Time and routine life cycles have a way of allowing the positive to erode and the negative to take its place.

This can be changed by catching each other doing things right and well. Catching each other doing things right and well builds confidence, morale, and causes people to focus on the positive things we do.

> **It seems our culture can be very negative, and mockery is something that is readily accepted.**

It is difficult to express the pain associated with these put downs. It brings up the idea of sarcasm. *Webster's* dictionary quotes sarcasm as *'to cut or tear flesh.'*[6] Our culture finds it interchanged with a joke which means everyone laughs. Sometimes cutting remarks are funny to all involved. If everyone does not laugh, it is sarcasm.

Sarcasm has collateral damage which means unkind remarks related to one person may be overheard by another, causing pain. An interesting thing about sarcasm is if you don't laugh, the next thing that you might hear is *"What's the matter can't you take a joke; I was only kidding."* This causes the pain to get you coming and going.

Jokes about yourself can usually ensure that it's not hurting someone else. Sometimes it's hard to laugh at ourselves, but it is extremely healthy in relationships. Being able to laugh at myself, tells me that I am confident in who I am and how I show up.

To foster healthy relationships, it is important to recognize the intent of the conversation. *Do I want to build this person up, or do I want to tear them down?*

It is important to recognize that there are multiple eras of relationship: when we first meet, after we're married, after children, children maturing in high school, children being launched to bring their families home to visit us and empty nesters.

How do we want to be treated by our loved ones during each of these life cycles? Am I being strategic and intentional about adapting myself in each of these time frames? Each is different and requires different skills.

As we accumulate resentments toward each other, we begin to major on each others minuses and overlook anything this done right and well. Compliments diminish and catching each other in error or making mistakes is inevitable.

These resentments create cesspools.

The more we point out each others minuses, the more the other person works on accumulating data against us and defending their position. The healthy way to identify if I am filling the cesspool or filling the heart is to begin to look at things I resent as opposed to things I appreciate. If I focus only on what is wrong or bad, the relationship will be set up for failure. Once we began to fill the cesspool with the negative thoughts, attitudes and actions we have collected on each other, we begin to rely on these as truths and continue to accumulate data proving their inability to be good in any way.

Lasting and emotionally mature relationships have more positive moments of connection than negative moments of disengagement. Feeling appreciated is one way of feeling pursued. If the act of pursuing and feeling pursued is missing, the relationship erodes. Finding methods of connection are ways of keeping us secure.

Filling the heart ensures that anxiety remains down, and intellect/spirituality is up. Filling the cesspool makes certain that anxiety will be high, intellect/spirituality will be down, and we will miss the million little opportunities to add value to each other. [BLIND SPOT]

No matter what we do, there are going to be misunderstandings, hurt feelings, and moments of disconnection in relationships. The methodology of filling the cesspool instigates sarcasm and resentment that tears us apart. Filling the heart makes us feel secure, important, and loved.

Land Sports versus Water Sports

A wonderful opportunity to seek change.

At times, we find ourselves at work, in war or in competitive arenas. In these arenas it is important to be right and win. In relationships, I encourage people to surrender to win. This does not mean to lay down at every disagreement, but to see if you can cause the other to feel good about themselves in the relationship.

Yielding to each other builds strength and comfort. Compromise improves trust and vulnerability, which produces healthy connections. Looking at the competitive arena and the relationship arena is like looking at land sports and water sports. The sports or activities I do on land, I cannot do effectively in the water. The water sports or activities I do are difficult, or perhaps impossible to do on land. What I do at work or in competitive arenas, which is all about winning, works well in that arena, but not in the arena of relationships.

> Sometimes the idea of surrendering to win can easily be seen by powerful people as being weak and unattractive.

Winning does not always look like gaining control and subduing the opposition. Looking for compromise, allowing the other person to have their point of view, being gently curious about what message they want us to understand about them and their thinking, will cause a joining and understanding that is not present in an argument. **When possible, allow others you love to be right and to win and expect the same in return.**

We hang out in what's familiar

Digging up old bones.

I hang out in what's familiar and not what's good for me. If it is familiar to be in a contentious relationship, it's easy to find myself caught in that familiarity, and it feels foreign to me when a relationship is smooth and easy. In a situation where going out of control to gain control is familiar, that's generally what I will do instead of being strategic and intentional about how to influence a kind and considerate environment. If love in our family was misconstrued as bad treatment, it is easier to hang out in bad treatment with the false impression that bad treatment is love. If love in our family was loyalty and devotion; that is what is familiar to me and is where I will hang out.

Sometimes in the work I do, I feel it is necessary to go back and dig up old bones of the past and sort them in a way that makes sense to the person who is wanting to change, understand, and appreciate how they became the person they are. Going back to change or rethink the way things were can help us, but sometimes it only causes more angst.

I use the term *'So what, now what.'*

This can sound somewhat cavalier, yet when I think about it, I know I can't go back and change the past. *So what,* the past is over. If I want to move forward, I now must look at the concept of *'now what.'*

What am I capable of doing?

What have I learned about my past?

What do I want to replicate?

What do I not want to replicate?

How do I want to show up?

What do I want others to say about me?

What do I want to say about myself?

So what, now what?

Just because they are family does not give them the right to abuse.

Habits and feelings are so powerful. Many times, I find myself feeling all the feelings I felt as a child, and I go back to that emotional place and act the way I did as that child.

If I had a harsh parent and would only get put down, told to be quiet, and show respect, I will react this same way if I feel I have upset the other person in my current relationship. This familiar feeling of subordination is carried forward. I resort back to acting the old ways of avoiding and going quiet when I really have a lot to say and need to get things out in the open. I am acting emotionally immature and am doing nothing but hurting the relationship.

If I shout out or say something in anger or in distress and it falls on deaf ears, then I feel like I have stated my case. If I feel it has been unheard, I take the attitude that it is not my fault, but it is your fault. I have told you what I need. I have told you what I want, and you do not listen. This brings me to the idea that as a child we learn how to handle stress in multiple ways, and we're not even aware that we are doing it.

When I am stressed, throw temper tantrums, use humor, placate, filibuster, or any other action or behavior and it causes stress to reside, I train myself inadvertently to do these things under stress. The question that I like to ask myself is, *"What would a mature adult do in this situation?"*

This allows me to rethink the way I respond, or the way I am going to handle this circumstance. If I have made a mistake and have gone out of control to gain control, what I want to do is go back to the person I was talking to and have the conversation. This conversation would begin with '*If I could do it again, here is how I would do it differently.*' It gives me so many opportunities, if such a circumstance should reoccur. I am working on better communications and building a better me in this relationship.

Talk about self when anxious and stressed

The buck stops here.

Many times, blame, ill will, deceit, and problem finding are used in a pejorative way. This kind of conversation in relationship ignites the other person. When I am accused of doing something wrong, my first response is the desire to prove them wrong. This puts me into defense or attack mode as opposed to an intellectual mode. I am choosing anxiety over intellect/spirituality. When I am accused, I get anxious. If I operate from my anxiety, I'll say or do things I will probably regret.

The change that I can generate here is to talk about myself only. This will cause tension or conflict to diminish and things to become more peaceful. When I talk about myself, there can be no argument. If I say you're manipulative, my thought is you'll tell me that you are not, and I'll go about trying to prove or convince you that you are. While you at the same time are trying to prove or convince me that I have the same or equal fault. If instead of saying you're manipulative, I say I'm allowing myself to be manipulated, suddenly, I have strength, courage, and insight to disallowing manipulation.

If you cuss at me and I blame you for cussing at me, I become a victim. If you cuss at me and I say to myself or out loud, *'I will not tolerate cussing,'* I am now in control of myself. I am teaching you if cussing persists, I will be absent. If I choose to be absent, I choose to be absent in a loving way. I love you too much to continue this conversation. I will return to continue this later.

Expressions that come up are: *"You're late,"* could translate into *"I was worried about you, or I was worried about your safety."* Statements like *"You're always working,"* could be reframed to *"I miss you dearly."* Anytime we use the word 'you' in an affirmative or complementary way, it is great.

If you are using 'you' in a negative way, it is received as conflictual.

When I want to yell, *"Why didn't you call?"* and cause an argument, I could refrain by saying:

"I'm so glad to see you."

"I was worried that something might have happened."

"I want you in my life."

"If something were to happen to you, I would be totally lost."

There are many examples of desiring to talk about the other person in a pejorative way that can be expressed in an affirming way. This can be motivating to me by reminding myself that I am the one who needs to take action.

When I blame, I do not have to change.

Anytime I blame, I can sit back and say, *"Life sucks because of you, I don't need to change, but you need to change."* But if I wait on you to change, I may wait a long time. I may teach you the way you're treating me is OK and I don't want to do that. I am going to influence change by continuing to talk about myself and not you in any conflictual conversation, thus diffusing anger and anxiety. Now I am allowing emotional maturity to be the intellectual force in the relationship.

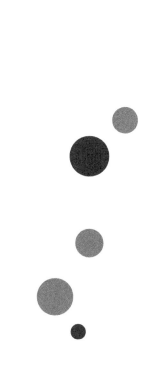

Anger can arise if I do not employ the principles presented here.

Listening is essential when it comes to diffusing anger.

I call anger the secondary emotion.
It is fueled by pain.

I say we are not angry unless we are hurting in some way. Physical pain or emotional pain can produce anger. If someone is standing on my foot, that can produce anger. If someone is saying negative or painful things about me or someone I love, that can produce anger. Something else to include in producing anger has to do with unfinished business, worries, fears or stressors that go unaddressed.

When I am worried about finances, my job, whether my car will make it to work, my inability to parent well, or any other life stressor, I am setting myself up to explode or be angry. At that moment, I'm totally unaware of it. I don't even know if that is going to happen.

Anger is also on a continuum from mild to chronic. We call it anger, but it is important to look where I am on this continuum for further clarification. Constant assessment of my emotional stability or ability is extremely important; otherwise, I find myself asleep at the wheel and acting out of emotions instead of intellect or spirituality.

When I go out of control to gain control, it is because I am feeling what I have done is ineffective. The only way to cause something to happen differently is to go into my reptilian brain, become loud and as big as I can, looking down on the other person, shouting and spitting as I speak and not even knowing, understanding, or appreciating the reason that I am anxious and not intellectual.

Carrying stress is carrying seeds of anger.

The more stressed I am, the more likely I am to show anger. I take

it out on someone who is subordinate to me. My anger is not the
same if I am in the presence of a policeman as it would be if I'm
talking to a small child. *Yipes that sounds awful.*

Again, under these circumstances of anger, it is important to look
at not only the sources of stressors, but the ability that I must go out
of control to gain control by allowing my emotions to get carried
away. When my emotions begin to escalate, my intellect/spirituali-
ty drops. I say and do the things when I am angry that cause me to
regret or apologize after I become more sane or intellectual. Under
these circumstances, the rational, reasonable, logical side of my brain
is totally inoperable. My anxiety is totally in control, and my frustration causes me to become horribly ineffective.

Many times, in my office I have sat on the floor and invited someone else who is going out of control to sit with me. An interesting
phenomenon of physiological change is fascinating when I see it in
action. I notice two things happen rather quickly. First, the amplitude
of their voice becomes much lower. Secondly, as they speak, the
context of their conversation also shifts.

This is one of the most remarkable things I have witnessed. When
stressed, I must not lose control of myself. That is emotionally
mature. Knowing what I want, what my intentions are, and acting
accordingly is extremely important. Otherwise, I am communicating
in a way that is totally futile. It teaches the one I am talking to that
the loudest, meanest, strongest get their way.

Subordination can over time lead to a broken spirit. A broken spirit
results in lack of confidence. It is not uncommon for one who hears
only the negative, time after time, conversation after conversation,
to feel unworthy. This is the person who always takes the back

seat and feels awful about it. It can be a source of shame. This is a person who learns by withholding information, anger is exposed.

There are numerous sources of anger and learning how to deal with them and admitting that we are angry, is an extremely healthy part of relationships. Too many times I see people, including myself, being blamed for being angry and want to defend their position or deny it because it is an ugly indictment. It is easy to argue, trying to show other circumstances or situations that are true, but are not addressing what the other person is trying to tell us in the moment. [See RMJ, page 70]

If we don't recognize anger, then we can do nothing but blame the other person. Sure, I am mad, but it is because of what you're doing. If you would not do these things, I would not be angry. I wonder how many of us have had that conversation.

Only I can control my anger.

Listening is essential when it comes to diffusing anger. Our hearing gets atrociously inadequate when we get angry. We do not hear ourselves, and we don't hear the other person. We can lessen the effects of anger by providing a safe listening space, asking gently curious questions, and allowing time to reframe our minds.

The secret to change is addressing what I want to see changed and what I can do to give what I say a chance. Too many times, I look for the other person to change, yet the only person that can change and create the situation that I am looking for is me.

Weekly Plan

Plan your week or it will plan you.

In the words of Stephen Covey...*begin with the end in mind.*[7]

How do you want your week to look?

How can you be strategic and intentional about causing what you want to have happen become a reality?

What happens if I set out on a journey and don't know where I am going?

Certainly, I may wind up in some lovely place or in an average place or in some place I truly don't want to be.

When I began the week with a plan, it doesn't mean that the plan should or will be carried out in full. A plan gives me a general direction of what I want to accomplish. It gives me an opportunity to declare my desires for accomplishments, relationships, myself, successes, and the difference I make.

What kind of attitude do I want to portray this week?

What do I want to leave as a legacy for the time I invested for the next seven days?

What do I want my faith journey to look like?

What do I want my work journey to look like? What do I want my relationship journey to look like?

What do I want people to say about me at the end of this week?

What do I want to say about myself at the end of this week?

Beginning a week without a plan is like starting on vacation not knowing where I am going. When I know how I want my week to look, I can be strategic and intentional, designing each day the way I want it to function.

I can prepare myself for tomorrow by doing things today or tonight.

I can set up rituals and routines that would cause me to be more productive, organized, and efficient. When I get up in the morning and my clothes for the day have already been laid out, my lunch already prepared, my breakfast prepared, and any normal morning chores completed the night before, I am ahead of the curve. I now have more downtime. I can better utilize my morning time for things like extra study, prayer, Bible reading, focusing on the things that make a difference. I can get up early in the morning, do my exercise, get to work, and have time to review my day and be sure that my daily plan will fit with the prescribed activities.

This kind of routine is very difficult to initiate. It takes small steps day after day, until these small steps become routine or habit. Once they become routine, I don't even think about them. It is no different than thinking about driving your vehicle. I don't get in and worry about what gear I put it in, when I use the blinker, when I need to change lanes, or how fast I need to go. I am on autopilot. It can become the same in my morning routine, thus allowing me to be more in control of my life. When I utilize my time efficiently by planning my week, I have more time to do the things that can make a difference.

How do you want your week to look?

Get your free downloadable weekly plan at
www.jerrydclark.com/weeklyplan

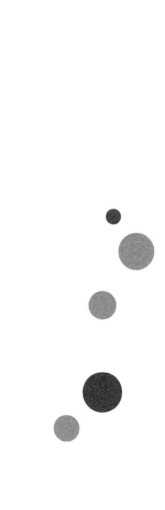

Calendar Night

 What's coming up...

Calendar night usually occurs on Sunday evening or night where parents take the calendar and look at what each family member must do for the upcoming week. At this point it is easy to talk about who will take care of what. Are there any events the parents can do together? It is time to look at any irregularities in work schedules that cause shifts in time or length of workdays. This is a good place to establish a date night and set up a time specifically reserved for the couple.

This calendar night to establish the week is strictly a 'plan' and is not cast in stone. If any deviations occur, it is necessary for both parties to be included. It is also a good thing not only to have a mutual electronic calendar, but also have one posted on the refrigerator or in the family room where it is accessible by either parent and the children. The children can be aware of what the parents have planned.

After the week has been planned specifically, then I suggest that you go out six to eight weeks in general and look for things coming down the pipe such as birthdays, holidays, anniversaries, celebrations of any kind in the nuclear or extended family. It is a great time to start an early conversation about these things coming up and begin to include them into your conversations. At the end of each calendar night planning, I suggest the couple ask these two marriage maintenance questions:

1) What do you need from me that you are not getting?

    Examples:

    You used to meet me at the door when I came
    home from work.

I miss your laugh and humor.

I liked it when we had conversation after we went to bed.

I miss us eating dinner as a family.

This question can be approached from a flippant point of view or from a relationship building point of view. I suggest it be used to build the relationship. Just because you ask, does not mean you will get. It gives each a straight away view of what is missing.

2) What are you not talking about that we need to be talking about?

Examples:

I was upset after our conversation on Wednesday.

I was upset when you forgot to call.

I did not tell you how much it cost. I was afraid you would be upset.

I was upset that I did not play golf/go shopping.

Clearing the air pertaining to what did not get said is crucial for healthy relations.

> **It is not what we say, but what we do not say that causes problems in relationships.**

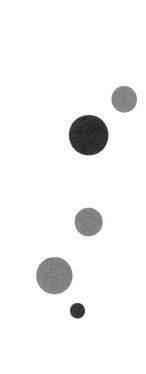

Wrapping Paper Exercise

Planning for the future, eliminating elements of surprise.

I suggest you build an instrument that allows you to look at the rest of your life on an annual basis. I call it the *'wrapping paper exercise.'* The instrument consists of 10 or 12 feet of birthday or Christmas wrapping paper.

Use the back side of this paper which is blank. It can be draped over the kitchen table. On the far-left hand side and in the middle of the page, write today's date. Draw a line from this date across the center of the paper to within 3 feet of the right side. At the end of the line, write your estimated expiration date. This part of the exercise usually represents a struggle because it is not only difficult to know, but also uncommon to disclose at least out loud. Although we don't know that specific time, look at the longevity of your family. How long have your relatives lived? How is your health? Once you put this date down and subtract today's date from your expiration date, you can see the number of years available for your plan.

Example: I suggest if you estimate you will live to 95 years old, that you subtract a few years perhaps 5 or 7, because if you have not done it by 88 or 90, it might not get done. Let's say you are 27 now and you expect to live until 95. If you take 7 years off, it leaves you the years between 27 and 88 for your plan.

At this point in time, it's important to become strategic and intentional to identify all the things that can be added to this 61 year timeline. Perhaps you are looking at starting a new family. This allows you to map your family on the timeline. If you already have young children that will start school, middle school, high school, or college, these dates can be placed on the timeline. You can estimate when you will be empty nesters. Identifying financial requirements like a new roof, air conditioners, cars, furniture, house, retirement, and other items relevant to you, can be located on the timeline according to dates they are needed. This allows planning for major expenditures and eliminates some elements of surprise.

If children are going to be driving in a few years, who's going to pay for drivers' education? When will the driver's license be allowed? Who is going to buy the car, pay the insurance, gas, and maintenance? At what point do you need to start teaching them about repairs and expenses associated with automobiles. What do kids need to learn before they begin to drive?

All of this sounds very simple, yet until you see it on a timeline, it is just hidden in your imagination. Having the answers to these questions before they are present is stress relieving. Anticipating these expenditures allows the opportunity to strategize and establish a plan to ensure things happen the way you want them to happen as best you can.

A friend of mine had four daughters in college age at one time. Long before these occasions happened, the parents looked at the idea of college and wedding costs coming up. They sat down with all of them together and explained to them how much money was available for each girl's total education and wedding. The girls were able to identify how they wanted to spend that money on these two major life events. They could choose college in or out of state. They could allocate wedding expenditures. The parents allocated their money according to their decisions at the time of the events.

This *wrapping paper exercise* can be used for so many considerations. You can graph what expenses will be associated with buying a car, putting kids through college. Highlighting things in the future will cause less financial and emotional stress.

> ## *It becomes a strategic tool to plan your future.*

This is extremely useful for young and older couples. It makes a difference if your children are still in the home or out of the home. Having this timeline filled in, representing your forecasted future, can be extremely important. It is noteworthy to look at what year you want to retire and at what income level you want after you retire.

After plotting as much information on this wrapping paper as you possibly can, you have a plan for your future.

Example: Take a hypothetical family of mom and dad at 27 years old and 3 children ages 2, 3, and 5, and then it becomes easy to add what is obvious with this family. They will attend school at 5 or 6, begin driving at 16, and graduate high school at about 18. They then go off to college and later bring their family home to your home.

It is significant to look at these life junctures because of the life cycles at these times. Life changes when children start school, begin driving, graduate high school, enter college, and begin to have their own families. If parents do not shift their parenting and thinking during these junctures, they will quickly be left behind by the growing children, adolescents, and young adults. An interesting phenomenon needs to be taking place during these years; children need to be learning how to become independent and parents need to learn to let go. There is a delicate balance determined by the physical, intellectual, and emotional maturity.

The hypothetical timeline diagram below can serve as an example of how your timeline might take shape.

Remember I asked you to leave about three feet on the right side of the paper? I suggest you divide this into three columns. In one column are her dreams of things she wants in her life. These dreams are not limited by time or money, just dreams of things that are of interest or passion for her. He does the same in the last column.

● Diagram 1—**Hypothetical Timeline**
   Serve as an example of how your timeline might take shape.

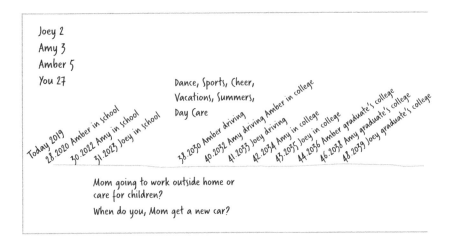

The middle column is for both to look at things that would be of interest and passion for the two of them together. This could be travel, animals, skydiving, flying an airplane, mission trips, new hobbies, and many more ideas. The list can consist of anything worth dreaming for. At the end of this exercise, the paper is to be rolled up and placed in the closet until next year when it is brought out, reviewed, and updated.

Utilizing this exercise allows you, your spouse and family to look at the rest of your lives on an annual basis and can aid in building hope and anticipation. It is not set in stone, but continually updated and collaborated on to meet the needs or changes that take place.

What do I want? My Dreams

YOURS	OURS	Mine
Own Property for horse	Home in the Rockies	Boat
Home in the country w/river	Visit Australia	Golf Cart
More horses	See Swiss Alps	New Truck
Riding Stables	Sailboat	Pilot's Liscense
Horse Rescue Facility	Trip to Iceland	Annual Fishing Trip
Dog Rescue Facility	and many more...	w/boys
Horse Training for Veterans		Write a Book
and many more...		Be physically fit
		and many more...

Weddings, Cars
Assist kids getting started
90:2081
95:2086

3 by 5 Cards

Prepare, Plan, Guide

There are many times I encounter someone who is markedly difficult in conversation. They are intensely imperceptible of their communication style.

This can be a spouse, an inlaw, or anyone who is somewhat intimidating. You may hear comments such as you need to keep your garage cleaner, you need to rearrange your cabinets, you need to pay more attention to the way you dress.

Sometimes it could be in the form of a question such as *"Why do you decorate so eclectically?"* These rather caustic statements or questions are sometimes met with resistance and put me on the defense. Regardless of what I say to defend myself, it is usually not enough, and it is easy to get caught up in a trifling conversation in which I do not want to participate.

It doesn't matter what I say, I feel like I'm going to be in trouble. *What are you doing that for? Why don't you come over? Why don't you ever return my call? Why do you spoil your children?* Any of these combative questions can be interpreted as being said out of kindness, but are experienced as caustic. Out of familiarity, routine habit, feelings of inferiority, it is easy to feel ambushed and retreat. If I answer, my words will be shot down.

As I dance back and forth trying to get my point across, the attacker usually is dominant because they struck the first blow, and I go away from the conversation feeling bad about myself and them. It is important to know that being kind, timid, embarrassed, or perhaps insecure causes me to explain too much even if I do not want to. Perhaps, I do not feel good about saying 'nothing.'

I love to use three by five cards to address this situation. I talked earlier about being clear and consistent and not convincing. When I go into convince mode, I lose myself and have conversations that the other person wants to have as opposed to my own agenda.

In reading the gospels of the Bible, Jesus has an impeccable way of dealing with attacking conversations. He has the ability to step aside and let the words go into the wind, and then talk about what he wants to say. He does this in a way as to not specifically answer the questions or engage in what they are asking, but in a way that is out of the ordinary. He usually tells a story or parable that is connected to their conversation, but is not what they are expecting to hear. His conversation is about their subject, but is not engaging them in a manner where He loses self-control. He shows up as a surgeon, dissecting their words or intentions and making new sense of what they are talking about. This is difficult to do without practice.

In using three by five cards, I like the idea of identifying something that a person might say or ask. Then at the top of a three by five card, I write down that question and the answer I would like to give when I'm in their presence. I think of another question or situation that might arise during that conversation and I get a new three by five card, write the question I expect to hear, and then the answer that I would like to give. I go through this activity considering any and everything I can think of. I even identify any circumstances that may occur, write them down and what action or response I want to employ.

To play offense, I might bring up something first to let them know I do not want to talk about a particular subject. I would do this in a kind and respectful manner, causing me to feel more confident in my communications.

I was talking to a friend who was going home to see his mother and was very apprehensive about the trip. He says that she always has an agenda which is extraordinarily negative, judgmental, and critical about everything going on in his life. She might be upset about politics, neighbors, or world circumstances. He is constantly dodging questions, trying to quail or satisfy his mother's volatile conversation about things in which she is not in charge and of which he is definitely uninterested. These circumstances can show up an any relationship.

My friend decided he would use his flight time to prepare his three by five cards. He spent several hours writing her questions, state-ments, his comments, and replies. When he arrived at his mom's house, the first conversation that she asked was overwhelming. He fell back into his old patterns of answering her questions, trying to convince her that what she was saying was not right and found himself quickly caught up in the old habits. He disengaged to rethink his new strategy.

The next day, he was able to implement the cards that he worked on during his flight. He brought up things before she brought them up. An example was going through old stuff in the home to sort out what needed to be kept or discarded. Instead of waiting for the question or the demand to help her, he brought up to her that they had enough conversation in the past concerning the old stuff. He reminded her that the old stuff had already been handled. He was not going to begin the trip by having that conversation. By providing this preemptive strike, she did not mention it at all and honored his request. He was very pleasantly surprised. When he shared his mother's reaction with his sister who lived in the same town, she was amazed.

I call this being on the offense rather than defense. On the offense, he was able to get his point across first, as opposed to waiting until she made a move and then having to react to her move. This went on for the rest of his visit. He was there almost a week. He designed what was going to happen and what they were going to do. If she brought up something that he didn't want to talk about, he politely suggested another topic. He reports that it was one of the best visits he has had with his mom in many years. Being intentional and strategic about who we are and how we show up in a conversation can cause connection as opposed to causing silent retreat, anger, frustration, criticism, or unrest.

I have found it important to be purposeful and prepared for these kinds of conversations. When I can anticipate what someone might say or ask and prepare a reply, I am much more capable of participating in a conversation that engages connection or at least minimizes disconnection.

Now I do not react from a defensive mode, but am offensive in my method of communications. Offense here does not mean attack; it means being strategic rather than being reactive.

I want to be in control of myself, my mood, and my presentation in conversation. The better I prepare for it and initiate it, the more I feel confident in my participation in the conversation. Before, it was exasperating to participate in such a lopsided dialogue. I found myself trying to defend or make sense to someone who already has their mind set on their truth of the situation.

Remember Jesus and His impeccable way of dealing with attacking conversations. Allow yourself to step aside and let accusatory words go into the wind, and then talk about what you want to say. Preparation sets you apart and guides you through intensely imperceptible communication styles. Three by five cards are the perfect solution.

The Hly Bible...

The Big Play Book

Knowing the contents of the Bible, God's Word, propels me into living a wonderful life. It is the best play book I have ever studied and drawn on. Based on where I am in my life, the meaning, or the contents of the Bible speaks to me differently. To set my standards by God's Word is to live in a manner that guides me spiritually and socially. Being able to relate to Him and the people He puts in my life is an amazing thrill and an ever-changing landscape. For me, the Bible is shifting and ever evolving depending on my place, circumstances, life, and the depth of my study.

Example: Paul was able to find joy in prison. Hearing this in my early life was inconceivable to me. I could never imagine finding joy being locked up with difficult people who didn't have my best interest in mind. Today, I see that there are many 'prisons' I find myself in where I can choose to find joy. Paul said *"I've learned by now to be quite content whatever my circumstances. Whatever I have, wherever I am, I can make it through…"*[8] That means I need joy, when I am stuck in traffic, waiting on someone, feeling like I don't have control, or in disagreement with someone I love. I like the following quotation from Darren Hardy's podcast *Darren Daily, "I can find my way through, change my frustrations into fascinations and be joyful."*

By no means do I know or understand all the things that are in the Bible. I am not a Bible scholar, but I do know when I live by the laws that are so well written in this book, my life works better, and I am a better husband, father, neighbor, and human.

My approach to the Bible and the Lord has been erratic until the mid to latter part of my life. Early on I was strong, courageous, bold, right, and in charge. This kind of thinking led me astray in many ways. Doing it my way is certainly not God's way. Over the years I've been so close and so far away from God in short periods of time. For the most part, I was close to Him when I was in trouble, and I was distant when life was going well. Maybe you can relate.

Today I base my life on living in a Christian manner. Doing the things I need to do to build a better me and to take good care of the people He has placed in my life.

In the last 25 years, I have recognized that God 'puts' people in my life. Some He wants me to take care of, and some He sends to take care of me. What a blessing. Thank you, Lord. Get into the best playbook ever written. Find joy and contentment in any prison that may arise to constrain you. Engage in a relationship with God's Word.

I love doing God's work. When I am called home, I want to have dirt on my hands.

Spiritual maturity is the backbone of my existence!

Tol Chest

Building a better you.

Many times, at the beginning of a session with couples I ask, *"How are things going?"* When I hear the comment *"Things are going well,"* I ask the gently curious question *"How come?"* It gives the couple an opportunity to assess the things they have been doing differently that have caused the relationship to improve.

This is an extremely important question simply because whatever the couple has been doing has caused the relationship to prosper and this needs to be documented. I call this document the 'tool chest.' It can be in a notebook, a diary or in the notes on your phone.

If we are being *honest,* there are times in the relationship when things begin to deteriorate—*again.* If the couple finds things are not going as well, this 'tool chest' is a great place to begin to assess what was being done differently when the relationship was flourishing. This is quick access to reorient when things are not flowing.

It establishes a foundation to improve the quality of your life and your relationships, building a better you. As you continue to evaluate, explore, and uncover your blind spots, jot down and make notes of what you feel are important treasures you have mined on this journey. These valuable, life-changing ideas and principles give you a unique viewpoint to modify your haphazard approach, to a well thought out and intentional application impacting who you are and how you show up.

This is just the beginning of limitless possibilities to your emotional health and maturity. You have identified destructive habits and behaviors causing problems in relationships, not allowing your anxiety to override your intellect. You have discovered and exposed hidden blind spots which will enhance your communication skills and allowed you to obtain the closeness in relationships you desire. You have seen how vulnerability can be frightening, yet you stand and remain undaunted with the courage it takes to change YOU.

Success will depend on you continuing to practice, document and empower yourself to build a better you. I suggest you establish your own 'tool chest' to quickly access the blind spots that you reveal and the things that you would like to alter. You are closer today than you were yesterday, so keep pressing on and remember the **Big Play Book** emphasizes that "above all and before all, do this: *Get Wisdom!* Write this at the top of your 'tool chest': *Get Understanding!"*

Keep looking for the blind spots!

Author Autobiography

My Journey

Growing up in West Texas was exciting. Cactus, mesquite trees and caliche roads were the scenery of the day. This doesn't sound too exciting or picturesque, but when you don't have anything to compare it to, it can be good enough. Traveling to the Rockies, as a kid, was over the top for me.

We were a very modest family of Mom, Dad, three boys and three girls. It was 1946 when I made my debut as the 5th child. Mom and Dad lacked education, but stressed it very strongly for us. I graduated Central High School in 1964 and entered San Angelo Junior College the following year. I did not know what *'Scholastic Probation'* supposed until I found out what *'Scholastic Suspension'* meant. [BLIND SPOT] This gave me the chance to join the Marines. So, in 1966, along with three of my friends, I left for San Diego, California.

I worked hard as a Marine Recruit and upon graduation from boot camp, I was awarded a set of *'Dress Blues'* as *'Platoon Honor Man.'* It also included a promotion and a trip to the Orient. I found myself as a Rifleman in Vietnam in early August of 1966. I returned home in late September of 1967 with no visible wounds of war. I got out of the Marines in 1968 and was married in 1969. My two sons were born within three years, and I was a very proud dad, but highly uneducated in that role.

I graduated in 1971 from Angelo State University. I was hired by

General Telephone company as a project manager and ended this career thirty years later as an Engineering and Construction manager. General Telephone Company changed names into GTE and then became Verizon.

As I said earlier, I did not know how to be a dad nor a husband but gave it my best. Needless to say, I was ill equipped to do either one effectively. After 13 years, our marriage failed. I did not recognize my contribution to the demise of the marriage until my second marriage began to take on the characteristics of the first. I attempted counseling but it was not for me, and it didn't work.

My second adventure in counseling was a very different experience. I was more focused on what I had to lose. It is a different experience to look for growth and a new approach to life that yields peace and calmness. It is fascinating to explore what I did not know about being myself. What a different journey to look at my actions and be able to accept them and even to laugh at myself.

It was during my career with Verizon that family problems brought me back into counseling, and it was during that time I felt God pulling me into a new career. It would take an intensive effort to transition into this new career, but I felt it was worth it. This was a life changing experience. I learned so much about myself and others. The emotional education was the biggest experience for me. I learned there are more emotions than happy and mad. Okay, so I was emotionally constipated, what can I say?

As I returned to college, I was working full time. It took a tremendous commitment to balance work, school, family, and personal life. I graduated with a degree and a wonderful education in Marriage and Family Therapy in 1996 from The University of Houston Clear Lake. I began working evenings and nights as well as on Saturdays. These hours worked for me and worked well for clients because not many therapists offered these hours. I was also working as an Intern at Devereux Hospital where I met many psychiatrists and therapists who were great resources for referrals during my early years.

I retired from Verizon in 1999 and have since experienced a wonderful career in counseling. I have been a lifetime Christian and have been a member of Bay Harbour UMC for the past 29 years.

My current plans include living the next twenty years leaning forward, making a difference in my own life and any others I can positively touch. I refuse to sit back and allow life to happen but to stay heavily involved with making a positive difference to myself and any others who will accept the challenge to look at their blind spots.

I learned from high school and my early years in college the importance of applying my talents and skills. The Marines taught me teamwork and that I could endure most anything from physical to emotional abuse. I knew then it was preparing me for the near future. Viet Nam taught me that life was precious and could be exhausted in a heartbeat. I left home a boy and came back an old man. I remember my dad saying before I left *"Jerry we don't want no heroes; we just want you back."* Oh, how they worried until I returned.

I learned from my corporate experience how and how not to manage people. I learned how to and how not to play the political corporate game. Through counseling, I have learned the best education of self-control and the impact of emotions in relationships.

My long and experienced filled life has been employed in my quest to contribute to healthy families. I know the experience of unhealthy ones. This book was born by the fact that I repeat the same message  daily. I want others to get the benefit of what I have been taught by the wonderful people who have courageously dared to enter the sacred room of therapy.

I pray great things for each of you and challenge you to drop the struggles of the past, lean forward, and create the best years ever in the remaining years of your life. God speed!

Notes

I have included a list of notes, references, and citations for the book. I trust that most readers will find this list to be sufficient. However, I realize that literature changes over time. I have listed what I believe to be the most recent information that is available.

Anxiety vs Intellect | pg 27

[1] *"Harris gets 20 years for Mercedes murder". CNN Justice. 2003-02-14.*

RMJ | pg 70

[2] *Take a look at what Webster has to say about each word...*
www.merriam-webster.com/dictionary/justify
www.merriam-webster.com/dictionary/rationalize
www.merriam-webster.com/dictionary/minimize

What do I want | pg 81-82

[3] Figure WD 1-2—**Weekly Display*** is a similar concept I utilize in my practice as, *The Weekly Rhythm Register,* in the *"Compound Effect"* hardcover by Darren Hardy, page 170. ISBN-10-0306924633 | ISBN-13 978-0306924637

What is the source of the problem | pg 116

[4] *"The Great Pretender" is a popular song recorded by The Platters, with Tony Williams on lead vocals, and released as a single in November 1955.*
https://en.wikipedia.org/wiki/The_Great_Pretender

I can only change myself | pg 126

[5] *Change is inevitable, growth is optional. ~ John C. Maxwell*
Listed is the factual evidence of an official source published by either the author, an author's representative or estate.
www.facebook.com/JohnCMaxwell/photos/a.321224427953.148
750.48357502953/10153969611402954/?type=3&theater

Cesspool vs Heart | pg 147

[6] *Webster's dictionary quotes sarcasm as: 'to cut or tear flesh.'*
www.merriam-webster.com/dictionary/sarcasm

Weekly Plan | pg 164

[7] In the words of Stephen Covey...*begin with the end in mind.*
The second habit Stephen Covey covers in *The 7 Habits of Highly Effective People* is
"Begin With the End in Mind." Personal Leadership Principles | *pg 95*

The Holy Bible | pg 185

[8] Paul said it, *"I've learned by now to be quite content whatever my*
circumstances. Whatever I have, wherever I am, I can make it through..."
www.biblegateway.com/passage/?search=Philippians%204%3A10-14
&version=MSG Copyright © 1993, 2002, 2018 by Eugene H. Peterson

Made in the USA
Coppell, TX
06 February 2022

72961268R00115